WHICH THE DAYS NEVER KNOW

A Year in Vietnam by the Numbers

Elephant's Bookshelf Press, LLC
Springfield, N.J. 07081
www.elephantsbookshelfpress.com

ISBN-13: 978-1-940180-90-8
Printed in the United States of America

WHICH THE DAYS NEVER KNOW

A Year in Vietnam by the Numbers

By Donald McNamara

Elephant's Bookshelf Press
Springfield, N.J.

Dedication

To the memory of anyone whose year was foreshortened because of the Vietnam conflict; but especially to the memories of William E. Cossa Jr., Walter L. Tiller, and Donald P. Davies, as well as to those of Joseph Oleson Jr. and the rest of the baker's dozen of young men who have streets in Bloomfield, New Jersey, named after them.

The years teach much which the days never know.
Ralph Waldo Emerson

So much of war is sitting around and doing nothing, waiting for somebody else.
Graham Greene, *The Quiet American*

After her parents died and her brother left for the underground, my mother lived alone, fretting and pacing through a whole year of days.
Duong Thu Huong, *Paradise of the Blind*

If we don't change direction soon, we'll end up where we're going.
Irwin Corey

A year by the numbers

T he standard tour of duty for a U.S. Army soldier in Vietnam was one year, an arrangement that caused many to regard their posting as a succession of days until they could return to what they referred to as the real world, rather than as one large enterprise.

The format of this book's year of numbered days is meant to reflect that state of mind, as well as the military practice of teaching by the numbers and of having numbers for just about everything. It is not intended as a straight memoir or autobiography, although, as with almost any writing, autobiographical elements will find their way in, and did. Certainly, recollections of experiences over time are present. Some names and characteristics have been changed (and some have not), some events have been compressed or rearranged, and some dialogue has been recreated, or just created.

This year of days is an attempt to view the conflict in a way that many participants had to view it: one day after another, knowing that an end was in sight but sometimes wondering if that end would ever come, and knowing — and at the same time denying — that the end could come in the most tragic way. As in a real year, some days bring an intense focus on the immediate situation and other days leave time for reflection or simple escape.

For the most part, this year sticks to facts (or factoids), but on this I presume to stand with the Irish playwright Sean O'Casey in declaring that it is the artistic truth that matters, not the literal. That is another way of saying that I have exercised my poetic license (and I actually have one, framed, even if I don't claim to be a poet) and made slight adjustments where I found such adjustments to be necessary.

Don't like it? What are you going to do, draft me into the military? Send me to a combat zone? Have somebody shoot at me? People don't always feel any different at the end of one year than they did at the end of the previous one, but over time we realize that we might be viewing the world, or ourselves in it, differently.

For a reader, that might happen at the end of this year, or it might take longer, or it might never happen. At any rate, my wish is that this trip around the sun proves to be gratifying.

DMcN

Day 1: One each

One day.
One year.
One war.

One life.

So many ones.

One small step.

35 and 10 equals I?
Green Bay 35, Kansas City 10.
Who knew?

First Aviation Brigade
First Cav (Airmobile)
I Corps
First Marine Aircraft Wing
First Marine Division
I Field Force Vietnam
Big Red One (Duty First)
First Logistical Command
First Signal Brigade
All on one side.

There was one other side.
Two sides.
One won.
One.

Day 2: Two brooms

Saladin's Blade

Di An

Afraid he wouldn't be busy,
they put a broom in his hand
and
told him to sweep the floor.
It was a big broom,
heavy,
strong,
with long bristles, tough bristles.
The newest and the best,
made with all American materiel,
meeting all the toughest production specs.
He swept the floor,
pushed the broom,
even leaned down
and pressed as he watched the broom
scraping across the cement floor,
loud.
He watched, too,
as the dirt he was supposed to be sweeping
moved lightly
around and over
the big, strong broom,
refusing to go where it was supposed to go.

And then, when he was finished,
along came a girl,
half his size,
with a broom she could hold in one small hand,
a lighter broom,
a softer one,

made carefully, lovingly, knowingly
of local material;
and softly and quietly
using less than half his effort,
she swept away all the dirt his big heavy broom had left.

Day 3: Three threes

Three meals.
At least they feed you.
Three meals a day.
Usually.
In basic and AIT
You could count the time until the next meal.
Can you do that here?
Breakfast, more
than you ever ate at home.
And lunch.
Or was it dinner?
And supper.
Or was that dinner?
It's chow.
Morning, noon, evening.
Hut, two, three.
So praise the Lord and pass the saltpeter.
But out in the field
a meal could be
Meal, Combat, Individual,
commonly (if inaccurately) called C-rations,
fresh out of a can.
Like meatballs and beans (What?! Oh yeah.)
or
ham and lima beans,
and who the hell's idea was that?

Followed by apricots or pound cake,
and cigarettes and gum in here somewhere.
Or sometimes it could be hot food,
Bought out by the mess sergeant
and served on a chow line.
But spread out when you line up;
one round could get all of you.

Three KIA.
By one claymore (Chicom).
One explosion, loud, with
flash, orange; smoke, black.
One grenade, smoke, purple,
on one belt, web,
giving out smoke, ironically,
not as intended, originally.

Meanwhile, three astronauts.
Killed in their own line of duty,
without even lifting off.
Didn't even get to 3 ... 2 ... 1.

Day 4: Four men

The four of them looked at each other,
as they searched for a place to sit,
four swingin' dicks
being sent into the inferno
waiting for the truck ride
to the chopper ride
to the jeep ride
to their new
"home"?
No. Posting. This will never be home.

"Hi," "How are ya?"
"Where you from in the real world?"
"I'm from ..."
Vermont
and California and
Washington
and Florida,
and St. Louis, the Gateway to the West,
and Puerto Rico,
and Alaska and Hawaii too.
From Philly,
and New Yawk and Dee-troit and Chi, and Cheyenne.
From Olde Towne and Newtown.
From North Fork and
Down South places
you never heard of.
They came from good homes and
bad homes and
no homes and
hey homes;
happy homes,
and sad homes,
and nobody's homes.
Fresh-faced (well, some),
young (most),
clean, sort of.
Johnson and DiGiovanni,
Janowski and ben Yochanon.
Johanson and MacOwen,
or McIan (dubh or any other color).
Dejean and Ivanovich.
Janzoon and DeJuan.
Džonsan and Djonson.
Jansana and Jōhnsananō.
Red, white, and
black, and brown, and whatever else there is,

even yellow.
Each beginning a year.
Will each of those years
reach 365 days?
Who will they be a year from now?

Another four
never left the safety of the USA.
Jeffrey Miller, Allison Krause, William Schroeder, Sandra Lee
    Scheuer.
Four dead in Ohio.

And of course
that's not counting
the deaths at Jackson State University,
Phillip Lafayette Gibbs and Earl Green,
killed 11 days later.
Only two this time,
so at least we're getting the body count down.

Day 5: 5 minutes

Weapon, ammo, claymore, grenades (frag and smoke), canteens,
    two (later three), socks (one holding C-rations).
Saddle up.

Day 6: Six

On the other side of the world,
they fought a Six-Day War.
Six days. Not bad.
Find out how they did it.
Over here, six ...
Well, there's a sergeant with a rocker underneath.

Some of them came over with the rocker.
Some came over much lower and will go home with it.
Some day, young man, this could be you.
Some day you could have a rocker under you.
To sit back and tell the grandchildren what you did in the war?

Day 7: A week

Seven days in a week.
That's Sunday that runs into Monday that runs into Tuesday that
    runs into Wednesday that runs into Thursday that runs into
    Friday that runs into Saturday that runs into Sunday that runs
    into ...
So fast that one day becomes the next
that you don't even know what day it is
because what day it is doesn't matter.
There is no Sunday, or Monday,
or Tuesday, or Wednesday, or Thursday,
or Friday,
or Saturday.
The jungle doesn't know what day it is
any more than you know what day it is when you're in the jungle,
any more than the jungle knows who you are.
What difference does it make
which day of the week it was when someone died?
What difference does a day make?
Thedaysbecomeoneanotherandbeforeyouknowitit'sthenextday.
The days go so fast.
So slow.

Day 8: Squad

This is a squad.
Squad leader.

Two team leaders, Alpha and Bravo.
Riflemen, two each.
AR, two each.
Grenadier.
This is a squad?
It's all we can get.
All we can get to fight an enemy we can't even see.
Impossible Dream?

Day 9: On with the show

Bob Hope made nine trips
to Vietnam,
bringing along an entourage of performers.
Troupers for the troops.
This caused mixed reactions
at home,
between people who agreed with him
about the war
and people who didn't (see later in the day).
But reactions among the GIs
Weren't too mixed
when Raquel Welch got up there
and danced.
No, the reaction there
was close to unanimous.
Nine's a lucky number for the Vietnamese,
and the guys who saw those shows
considered themselves pretty lucky.

On the other side of the showbiz aisle,
there was a play
taking a completely different show on the road,
bringing Fun, Travel, and Adventure
to the left coast,
courtesy of Jane Fonda

(she of the antiaircraft weapon),
et al.

And then,
there was
The Catonsville Nine,
written by Dan Berrigan, S.J.,
one of the nine who went on trial
for taking yet another kind of show on the road.
A different set of footlights
for the (not-yet-to-be) troops,
many of whom
were not as appreciative
of the effort.

Day 10: Number 10

First lesson in speaking Vietnamese.
Start with "Numbah 10."
That's Vietnamese?
Well, it's Vietnamese by way of us.
Means "bad."
Looks bad, feels bad, smells bad, is bad.
Not good at all.
"Numbah 1" means "good."
(So, what's the deal with 9? Who knows)
So imagine, if you dare,
what "Numbah 10-thou" means.
Now that's bad.

And don't even get me started
on "beaucoup" and "titi"
or "didi mau."
Sorry about that, GI.

Day 11: MOS

Everyone in the military has an MOS.
Military Occupational Specialty.
In the Army, an MOS that started with 11
Was very popular.
That's "popular" in the sense
that a whole lot of guys had it.
And that's because
an MOS that started with 11
meant infantry,
The Queen of Battle,
and there were a whole lot of guys
in service to the queen.
There was 11B, light weapons infantry,
and 11C and 11H, and they worked with mortars.
Either way, it was infantry,
but it could make a difference for the humping
they had to do,
or what they had to carry when they did the humping.
It also made a difference for what they had to do
At night.
Because those 11B guys were more likely
to go out on a listening post
(or LP)
or an ambush patrol
(or AP or bushwhack),
but the 11C guys usually stayed back
for other things.
Like firing mortar rounds,
for harassment and interdiction,
also known as H&I.
But either way, they earned a CIB.
The Combat Infantry Badge.
Silver and blue.
That had to be camouflaged

for the jungle.
But still, it was a CIB,
and it meant something to the ones who wore it.

Day 12: The Playmates

We got 12 months in a year,
and each month a new issue of *Playboy*.
And each *Playboy* has a centerfold.
Playmate of the Month.
So someone got the idea
to take out the centerfold
and tack it up on the top of the wall of the hooch.
One a month.
Until, when we had a year of Playmates,
it was time for us to go home.
And the next guys could decide
if they wanted to start their own, or continue ours.
Twelve months, twelve pictures, twelve women.
And twenty-four ...
Twelve women to smile at us, to take our minds off
the heat and the sweat and the dirt. '
Twelve women to remind us of home,
and to make us think they would be waiting
when we got home.
The girls of our dreams, wet or dry.
So at least the top of the hooch was looking pretty good.

But
They were only pictures,
and we would never meet them,
and a month can be a long time to wait.
For the women we did meet, though,
take a look at Day 75.

Day 13: On the road again

Route 13 runs north from Saigon,
up there to An Loc or Loc Ninh or someplace.
It was called Thunder Road.
Hitting all the exotic spots:
Phu Cong, Ben Cat, Lai Khe, Bau Bang,
and various lesser-known locales.
It's a main road, a highway,
although "highway" here might not mean
what it would mean back in the world.
A dirt highway?
But still, they use it every day,
the Vietnamese. For business, commerce.
We use it too.
Not for business exactly.
And the NVA harass us when we do use it.
It runs right through the middle of the base,
kind of like Main Street.
Main Street that needs us to do mine sweeping
and security points.
Try to get a ride if you were walking on it.,
Like the time on the back of a jeep
that bounced so hard you fell out, but,
thanks to a couple of beers earlier on,
didn't feel a thing, just rolled with it.
Or the time the guy tried to run over a viper
that was almost as long as the road was wide,
and the crazy fucker missed and backed up to try again.
Try again!?
And I'm sitting in the back of the jeep.
Why don't we just keep going?
Never held on so tight.

And then up there a ways, in An Loc,
there was a beautiful stadium, for soccer, or whatever they played

when there was no war going on.
Maybe the French built it, who knows?
A sports stadium,
right there in the middle of a war.
Alongside a highway, such as it was.
No malls, though.
And what's a highway without malls?
But if you think that was crazy,
how about the railroad tracks in the middle of the jungle?
Yup, that too.

Day 14: Fourteen ways to leave your health

Didja know?
There are fourteen diseases recognized by the
     Veterans Administration
that are connected with the use of Agent Orange—
Herbicide Orange (HO) and Agent LNX,
a 50-50 mixture of 2,4,5-T
and 2,4D—during Operation Ranch Hand (that of Day 123).
Yup. Fourteen.
Who woulda thought
there could be such variety,
such diversity?
Look at all the possibilities.
AL Amyloidosis,
Chronic B-cell Leukemias,
Chloracne (or similar acneform disease),
Diabetes Mellitus Type 2,
Hodgkin's Disease (but we also got a non-Hodgkin's type—
     see below—just to be fair),
Ischemic Heart Disease,
Multiple Myeloma,
Non-Hodgkin's Lymphoma (see, I told ya),
Parkinson's Disease,
Peripheral Neuropathy, both acute and subacute (just trying to be
     fair again),

Porphyria Cutanea Tarda,
Prostate Cancer,
Respiratory cancers,
and
Soft Tissue sarcomas (other than osteosarcoma, chondrasarcoma,
     Kaposi's sarcoma, or mesothelioma, of course).

Our deeds live on, however.
Because
Our children can get
Spina Bifida.
That's a disease that occurs when the spine fails to close properly
     during pregnancy.

But we ain't finished. Not at all.
Let's not forget the feminine mystique.
It seems that at least eighteen birth defects—18—
are linked to a mother's experience in Vietnam.
But hold on now.
Those eighteen, they're not linked to herbicide exposure.
No sir, ma'am.
Whew! What a relief.

But don't go away
At this fortnight mark.

Before the M16 (see two days from now),
There was the M14.
That was the heavier one, the bigger one, the wooden one,
the one they carried in basic training.
The one that fired the NATO round,
although NATO wasn't too eager to be associated with this war.
It was the one that worked even in the heat
and dirt.
But it wasn't as good.
Because it wasn't the M16.

Day 15: Senatorial courtesy

A lot of politicians
(a LOT)
were in favor of the war,
but some were not.
In January of 1966,
15 senators sent a letter to President Johnson,
suggesting, merely,
that he refrain from resuming bombing of North Vietnam,
(he had ordered a break in the bombing for Christmas)
and continue to explore
a possible diplomatic settlement.
The leading signer
was Vance Hartke,
Democratic senator from Indiana,
and soon-to-be former good friend
of LBJ.
Another signer was Eugene McCarthy,
junior senator from Minnesota,
of whom more was destined to be heard.
Oh yeah,
LBJ ignored them
on both counts.

Day 16: M16

This is your weapon, infantryman.
It is a lightweight,
semiautomatic or automatic,
gas-operated,
magazine-fed,
(two-)hand-fired weapon.
You be good to it ...
"The Black Beast"

The weapon that is going to win the war.
As long as it doesn't get dirty,
in a place where the dirt is everywhere,
or get wet,
in a place where it rains all day half of the year,
or wear out,
even though its parts can't handle constant use,
or use the wrong powder
(that there "failure to extract" thing).
And while you're at it,
Take a look at Day 18.
But wait until the new version comes along.
If you can hold on until Day 177.
Now that will be the one that will win this war.

Day 17: DMZ

Back in Geneva,
where the weather isn't like in Vietnam,
they gathered,
in 1954,
British and Soviet and American and French and Chinese
representatives.
Even though the USA was there unwillingly.
And even Vietnamese—two delegations,
and Laos and Cambodia.
And because they couldn't decide
which was the real Vietnam,
they made two of them, and
they set up a demilitarized zone.
Or DMZ.
Now this wasn't meant to be permanent,
(and sure enough it wasn't).
It was at the 17th parallel.
That's parallel to the equator,

but 17 degrees north of it.
Except most of the zone lies south of the parallel.
Anyway, they made that the border
between the North and the South,
and then said no one could fight there.
So the VC could attack and then pull back
past the DMZ,
but we couldn't cross it,
with troops.
Because this wasn't a war.
It was a police action.
But we did send artillery rounds
from our fire support bases.
They was some who talked about
a fortified electronic barrier,
but that never went anywhere
(the talk or the barrier).
But check back in five days.
So we sent airplanes over it
with bombs
that didn't seem to make much difference.
At least in terms of helping us.
And some fierce fighting
took place in places near the DMZ.

Day 18: 18 rounds

So you put 18 rounds
(that's bullets to civilians)
in the magazine
(can't call it a clip)
of your M16.
That clip
(we're out in the field now, that rule doesn't apply)
was meant to hold 20 rounds,

but the weapon
(can't call it a gun, that rule still holds)
jams too easy with a full clip.
So you put in 19,
but you can't put in 19
because then the top round will be on the left, and that will jam
    the weapon.
It's the new applied math.
So you put in 18, and that way
it doesn't push too hard,
and doesn't start from the left,
so you're two bullets short,
but otherwise you're all set.
Unless the weapon still jams
because we're in a muggy climate,
and that isn't what they were meant for,
and it can get dirty easily and
they can't work if they're dirty,
and it's the wrong type of powder in the rounds,
and they're being pushed and pulled by a white bolt that wears out.
Keep your cleaning rod handy.

Day 19: The age of youth

The average age of a soldier
in Vietnam
was 19.
Except it wasn't.
That was just the urban (urban?) legend.
The average was higher,
if nothing else, because
of all the older guys.
But 19 was a big favorite anyway.
Those 19-year-olds
predominated the draft lists,

and when the draft lottery went into effect
it was to determine an order
for 19-year-olds.
So 19s get in there in a big way,
somehow or other.

Day 20: The Twenty Years War

"It was twenty years ago today
Sgt. Pepper taught the band to play."
So who's this Sgt. Pepper?
I never had any sergeant named Pepper.
And none of our sergeants
taught any band to play.
Imagine, if you can,
That there is music, and clothes that are some color,
other than OD.
Or a life that doesn't include a draft,
or a decision about a war,
or a girl singing a song like "Soldier Boy"
But twenty years ago,
that's counting 1955,
when MAAG, Vietnam
—later to be MACV—
(we'll see more of this)
was separated from MAAG, Indochina,
rather than the "official" Year One,
or 1965,
is what we can say
about the beginning of this war—
the longest in U.S. history,
believe it or not—
at the end of the war.
Twenty years.
And where

did that time go?
Oh, and 20-year-olds?
A total of 11,989 of them
died over there.
That's easily the Number One spot,
far outpacing 21-year-olds,
who came in Number Two with
7,953.
And those whipper-snapper 19-year-olds
came in at 7,015.
Just in case you were wondering.

Day 21: The Flying Banana

The H-21C,
later the CH-21C,
also known as the Flying Banana.
It was a twin rotor transport helicopter,
the most common transport chopper
in the early years of the war.
So nicknamed because
it looked like,
well, a flying banana,
except not yellow.
Sort of V-shaped,
like what artists use
to show birds far off,
but asymmetrical,
sort of like far-off birds seen from an angle.
It was originally designed
for cold weather,
so, yeah, that was a problem.
Made a heroic effort,
but it couldn't carry as many people
as it was supposed to,

and it was slow.
Still, it was a workhorse,
until around 1964,
when other craft took over most of its work.

Day 22: North and south

History lesson.
It took 22 years
to divide Vietnam between north and south.
22 years?
Yes, but this was from the 17th century.
When the Trinh dynasty,
which controlled the northern half,
fought the Nguyen dynasty,
which controlled the south.
They battled each other for a while.
And then in 1650,
the Nguyens made a series of attacks
on the Trinhs,
who fought off the attacks,
and then tried attacking again,
to no avail,
and after 22 years
they all said
the hell with it,
let's have a truce and divide the country.
And that's what they did.
If you don't know this about Vietnamese history
don't feel too bad,
because neither did anyone
who made decisions about
sending U.S. troops
into Vietnam.

Day 23: Walking the walk; the Valley of the Shadow of Death

The 23rd Psalm says:
"Though I walk through the valley of the shadow of death,
I will fear no evil,
for You are with me."

The soldier's version goes:
"Though I walk through the valley of the shadow of death,
I will fear no evil,
for I am the evilest son of a bitch in the valley."

Take your pick.

The 58,000-plus who didn't come out
the other end of that valley,
maybe fearing evil,
maybe not.
Did they find green pastures
or restful waters?
We can only hope.

Day 24: A soldier's home

Just to give you an idea
of where you are,
in relation to the real world, as it were,
think on this.
The northern border of North Vietnam,
that's with China, by the way,
is at roughly 24 degrees longitude.
That's right near the top of the Tropic of Cancer,
for those of you keeping track of your tropics.
That is about the same longitudinal line

as Key West.
Yeah, that Key West,
the one at the very end of U.S. 1
in Florida.
On the other side of the globe.
Now don't you feel better for knowing that?
And that's today's geography lesson.

Day 25: Pick 25

A hot day.
When the PRC 25, or prick 25,
Radio, walkie-talkie, whatever you want to call it,
is quiet.
Which is probably just as well,
because when the shooting starts
that antenna can be a target.
But it wasn't one of those days.
It was a quiet day at the NDP.
And a hot one.
A cold Coke.
They keep them cold in straw.
Don't ask me how the hell they do that.
And the going price is 30 p.
We don't speak their language,
and they don't speak ours.
So to indicate the price
they hold up three fingers.
Each finger is 10 cents, or piasters, or p,
or whatever you want to call them.
And if they want to indicate 5 cents (or see above line)
they hold one index finger crossways over the other.
Sort of indicating half. Got it?
So this one GI asks them how much they want for a Coke.
They all hold up three fingers.

Then he says, "Look, all I've got is 25 p
(and to prove it he shows them
all the MPCs—military payment certificates, if you must;
paper money, different sizes and colors
he has, and then does the thing with the fingers).
Will anyone sell me one for 25 p?"
No one moves. A few heads shake.
Then, as he is just about to give up,
comes a voice from the back of the crowd.
It's an old woman, pushing her way forward,
calling to let him know she'll sell him one for 25 p.
Then all the others chime in.
They'll sell it for 25 p also.
And they even press the bottle against his arm
to show him how cold it is.
But he gives his business to the old woman
Because she was the first.
And so it's 25.
For a cold drink.
Fresh from the "Brasseries et glasseries del Indochine."

Day 26: M26

An M26 is a fragmentation grenade.
A frag grenade.
The very latest in hand-wielded death.
It could travel as far as someone could throw it,
and its effective radius was 15 meters,
You pull the pin and throw.
Once it leaves your hand, the handle flies off.
That's when you have 4-5 seconds
Before it goes off.
But,
if you put that pin back in before the handle comes off,
the pin secures the handle, and no harm done.

You can keep doing that all day,
As long as you don't let the pin fall out
or the handle fly off.
Because if that handle flies off and you're still holding the grenade,
you're fucked,
or just dead,
not to put too fine a point on it.
Anyway, with its coiled spring around an explosive charge,
the M26 was considered an improvement
over the old pineapple grenades
that were left over from WW II and Korea,
but which still appeared in this jungle war.
Yup, we got to throw the same grenades
that John Wayne would have thrown
if he really threw any grenades.
Except the ones he threw worked.
What?
They were given these pineapple grenades,
that came in round boxes that said "1945" on them.
And they were told to drop them in tunnel entrances
as they walked past them.
So this one guy drops his pineapple.
Nothing happens.
Guy after him drops his pineapple, figures that'll get them both.
Nothing again.
What's going on here?
Third guy comes up.
"What's wrong, fellas?"
They tell him.
No problem. He'll drop his pineapple.
Nothing happens again.
So now we're going Godot one better.
So finally, they drop a new one, hoping that will set all of them.
It went off. Did it set off the others?
Who knows?
Nobody was waiting around to find out.

But even with the new improved version,
There could be a problem about those pins.
They were attached to a ring
that could snag on things like branches and vines and bushes.
And Viet Nam had a lot of those.
So eventually they came out with the M61,
Which couldn't snag.
See what a difference it made?

Day 27: Don't miss the link

You're not going to believe this,
but those disposable links
that connect the rounds for the machine gun,
they have a number.
It's M27.
And they can go on
forever.
Guess there's a number for everything
in this (???) man's Army.

Day 28: Domino, theory

See how they fall, or not.

Your basic domino set
has 28 pieces,
also called bones.
Not much of a skeleton,
but it makes one great theory.
Didja know
dominoes were first mentioned in China's Song Dynasty,
(great album, hard to find,
from 960 to Kublai Khan)?

Well they were.
And they were mentioned in
the good old US of A,
because countries would fall
like dominoes
if they weren't propped up.
So we propped up a domino.
But,
and you'll like the irony of this,
instead of our boneyard being cleared out,
it was filled up.

Day 29: Like, wow

It seems
a 1967 study found that
29 per cent of returning service members
admitted smoking marijuana
(that's the ones who admitted it),
at some time during their year over there,
although
(sigh of relief)
only 7 per cent did so more than twenty times.
Of course
by 1969 the number of total users was 50 per cent,
with 30 per cent in the "heavy use" category.
Now that's heavy, man.
And,
by 1971 it was 58.5 per cent.
From 50 percent to 58.5 percent,
now that's progress.
I can see a light at the end of the tunnel.
At least I think that's a light.
I mean, it sort of looks like a light,
you know what I mean, man?

The light's fading.
I better have another hit.

Day 30: 30 days

That's a month (close enough).
Take all those days that ran into a week,
and then those weeks ran into a month.
It's a month already.
Already?
A month of heat
and sweat
and dust
or rain
and war.
How long can a month last?
Real long. This long.
Only eleven more to go.
Eleven more months?
Someone told me the first day
"You never get used to it.
They tell you you do, but you don't."
He was right.
I'm not used to it,
and I won't ever be.
How will I stand it?
A month that feels like a year?

Day 31: Setting the bar

It took 31 points,
out of 100,
as the minimum on the test
to qualify

for the military.
Doesn't seem like a lot to ask,
but apparently quite a few guys
of draft age
were able to come in
under the bar.
Like in life,
some had to work hard at it,
and some found it coming to them easy.

Day 32: Down to Yasgur's farm

From Richie to Hendrix,
32 acts
by the time it was over.
Being part of something
bigger than they ever expected.
Half a million people,
much more than was ever planned,
gathered to listen
at an Aquarian exposition.
Everything ran out,
and as if that wasn't bad enough,
it rained
a lot.
But it was still memorable.
Somehow.
People said,
What the hell,
let's just go with it.
And they did.
The bands had to be brought in by chopper.
Now *there's* irony.
Armed with instruments
of music,

not of war.
But they got there.
The bands played.
The people listened.
The police
helped out when they could
and stood back when they couldn't.
Half a million people
in Bethel, New York.
Not possible.
How did they ever do it?
You really had to be there.

Day 33: Comfort Woman

Lai Khe

Some of them smile when they walk in,
Some of them laugh.
Some look like they will never smile or laugh again.
The fans
almost move the air
in here.
They sit.
They relax.
They have come in from the field
where they found the enemy
and lost friends.
They come here for comfort.
Do I give them comfort?
Comfort, woman.
Did they get comfort at home?
Have they found comfort here?
Where do I turn for comfort?
One walks in slowly, more wearily than the others.

Is he looking for comfort?
He drinks from a bottle, cold, water trickling down the sides,
The bottle sweats,
just like he does.
And someone says to him,
"How many days, short-timer?"
He lifts the bottle, showing the label: 33.
Ba Muoi Ba.
I look down at my badge, and that is my number.
33. That's me.
His smile is not as wide as that of the one
who asked him, who has a fresh-faced friend
who says, "I still can't believe it's legal here."
He has 33.
I have
"Saigon tea, hundred p"
and the rest of my life.
He reaches into his pocket,
Takes out his money and shows it to me.
From somewhere far off,
right in front of me, I hear "Short-time?"
I get up and go with him.
He puts aside his 33.
As I will put mine aside.
He leaves the discomfort of his fears, his nightmares.
I bring my body with me.
With this I give him comfort.

Day 34: USS Liberty

34 crew members were killed
and 171 wounded
when Israeli airplanes attacked
the USS Liberty
in the Mediterranean.

Israeli? Mediterranean?
It was during the Six Day War,
in 1967,
and there seems to have been
some kind of mix-up.
We were a neutral country,
just observing,
but something went wrong.
War just seems to find its victims.

Day 35: Dustoff

The announced time for a dustoff
was 35 minutes
from battlefield to medical attention,
so they could be attended inside an hour.
They often got it done
even faster than that.
Those Hueys swooping in
loading up
and getting them out of there
At great risk
to their own lives.
Who knows how much worse it would have been
without them?
Well, supposedly, 19 percent of the wounded died.
That compares to 33 percent in the Civil War,
29.3 percent in The Big One,
and 26.3 percent in Korea.
And, as near as anyone can tell,
the difference was those choppers.

Day 36: No job is finished until the paper work is done

36 people worked on what would become the Pentagon Papers.
These were documents showing how
some of the decisions regarding our decisions about Vietnam
weren't exactly the same
as the American people had been told.
A guy by the name
of Daniel Ellsburg
thought people should know
about those decisions.
And Nixon went to great lengths to prevent their publication,
even though they weren't about his decisions.
So why'd he get so hot and bothered?
Who knows?
Another mystery of the Orient.

Day 37: Best-laid plans

OPLAN 37.
That was the name usually given to OPLAN 37-64,
or Operational Plan 37-64.
It had three phases, the third of which was for "graduated
    overt pressure."
The plan that would win the war.
37 was also the official age of Army Major Dale Richard Buis,
the first name on the wall,
right there with master sergeant Charles (or Chester) Ovnand
    (the Wall says Ovnard)
(he was 44),
the second name,
although they are not the first official American KIAs
in Viet Nam.
That is Air Force technical sergeant Richard B. Fitzgibbon Jr.,

who died in 1956,
and was followed by his son,
Marine Lance Corporal Richard B. Fitzgibbon III,
who died in 1965.
Dale Buis had a wife and three sons in the States when he left.
They were still there when he didn't come home.
1956? 1959? That's affirmative, over.
Before OPLAN 37.
Before very many Americans had ever heard of Vietnam.
Except maybe the Buis and Ovnand families.
Oh plan.

Day 38: P38

For the army that moves on its stomach,
don't underestimate
that old 38.
Once there was a .38 caliber pistol.
Didn't do the job.
But there was a 38 that did do the job.
With all the equipment
a GI could carry,
all the weapons, ammunition, grenades,
mines, LAWs, whatever else,
one of the most important
is the good old 38.
That's the P38,
the can opener for C rations.
One small piece of metal,
not much bigger than a coin,
and probably lighter,
you'd hardly notice it.
Until you needed it.
That one little piece of metal—
it's even hinged to fold flat—

is what opens all those cans of C Rations.
Just pick it up, put it on the edge of than,
a few flicks of the wrist,
and there is the food,
ready for you to dig in.
Thanks to that little P38.

Day 39: Never ending

The last battle of the war,
wasn't even fought in Vietnam.
The Mayaguez,
Which wasn't a Navy ship
but a merchant ship,
with a crew of 39,
was seized by the Khmer Rouge
(and it's not for nothing that the "Rouge" is there)
in international waters
on May 12, 1975.
President Ford
(how many presidents did this war go through?)
Ordered a military rescue,
Which took place,
Except that by the time our military got there
The crew had been released.
The crew came out of it all right,
But 18 American servicemen didn't.
Their names were the last
put on the wall (original go-round).
and that includes three Marines,
who were captured
and executed.

Day 40: You go, Girl

Vietnam's troubles
with other countries
go way back.
In the year 40,
AD, CE, AC/DC, LSD, whatever,
(and just for reference, Caligula was The Man in Rome,
London was three years away from being bridged,
and Saul was five years away from Damascus),
the Trung sisters,
Trac and Nhi,
led an insurrection
and drove the Chinese out,
establishing independence.
It lasted two years,
until the Chinese came back
with a vengeance.
Trac and Nhi killed themselves,
rather than be taken prisoner.
So now,
in 1960,
South Vietnam is being run (feel free to insert judgmental adverb
     here)
by a guy named Ngo Din Diem,
who never married,
but whose sister,
Madame Ngo Din Nhu,
or Madame Nhu to you,
considered herself to be:
the First Lady of (South) Vietnam,
(although *Ramparts* considered her
the Dragon Lady of Saigon
and
very likely coordinator
for the entire

domestic opium traffic in Vietnam)
and,
the reincarnation of the Trung sisters
both in one, as it were.
She even had a statue honoring them
built in Saigon in 1962.
Madame Nhu retired to Rome
after her brother-in-law and husband
were killed in a coup.
Maybe they were the reincarnation of the Trung sisters.

And that issue of *Ramparts.*
It featured a picture of Nguyen Cao Ky on the cover,
wondering if he was the world's biggest pusher?

Day 41: Bylaws of the vanguard

41 articles were included
in the People's Revolutionary Bylaws,
the bylaws
of the People's Revolutionary Party,
or the "Marxist-Leninist Party of South Vietnam."
It was founded on January 1, 1962,
because
"to fulfill their historic and glorious duty, workers, peasants and
    laborers in South Vietnam need a vanguard group serving as a
    thoroughly revolutionary party."

Day 42: Boston proper, Boston common

Dorchester, Mass.
It's actually part
of the city of Boston.
Bigger than a neighborhood

but smaller than a city.
Anyway,
42 guys from there
were killed in the war.
Surrounding towns,
that weren't quite so, uh, blue collar,
had different numbers.
For example,
Milton, Lexington, and Wellesley,
which had populations about the same
as Dorchester,
had 11 KIA, combined.
But that's pretty much
the national story,
isn't it?
And how 'bout this.
After 1924, the Boston Marathon was 42.195 kilometers.
What goes around
goes around.

Day 43: Room service might not be too good, but security is great

43 people went to jail
by the time the whole Watergate thing shook out.
How the hell
can a half-ass break-in
in a hotel in Washington
affect our approach to a war in Southeast Asia?
Don't know,
but it did.
Life sure is strange,
isn't it?

Day 44: 44 provinces

South Vietnam,
the Republic of Vietnam, RVN,
had 44 provinces.
44 areas in which to win
hearts and minds.
The hearts and minds of the people
we're walking all over.
44?
Can we go for hearts in 22 and minds in 22 others?
And get this if you're into numbers:
44 was the number of states Johnson won in 1964,
in our winner-take-all electoral vote system.
How 'bout that?

Day 45: 45 caliber

The Gun that Won the West.
Okay, so maybe the .45 automatic,
officially the M1911, to keep it military,
that some carry as a sidearm
isn't exactly what the old sheriffs
and marshals carried,
but it still stands tall.
Makes a handy sidearm.
But maybe it won't clean up
the Southeast
like it did the Old West.
Three safeties.
Half-cock,
the correct grip
around the handle, not the barrel
and the safety.
Three ways of making sure

you really want to fire that shot.
For a weapon that might not shock and awe
like the latest big stuff,
it still can blow a hole
and knock back what it hits,
better than that old .38.
It's reliable, doesn't need
special treatment.
It's a handful.

Day 46: Sea Knight

The CH-46 was a helicopter
used by the Marines,
called the Sea Knight.
Could move upward
at 2,000 feet per minute.
It could carry heavy loads,
and it did.
It should not be confused
with the CH-46A,
which had a lot of problems.
No, the CH-46D worked pretty well,
which seems only right,
considering the Marines had to do some of the hardest work
    during the war.

Day 47: AKA

AK47.
That's the rifle they use, the enemy.
The ones who aren't using rifles
made from a hunk of wood and a pipe
or a carbine or an M1 or a BAR,
or whatever else they could get.

It's a Russian rifle.
Designed by Mike Kalashnikov.
Direct from the Soviet Union
or Russia, whatever.
Maybe not so direct.
Is it better than what we have?
It doesn't have a semi-automatic setting,
only automatic.
But,
they don't have to carry a cleaning rod with it.
Because it doesn't jam.
That sounds good to any infantryman.

On our side,
the CH47 was the Chinook helicopter ,
that big thing with blades at both ends,
kind of like the Sea Knight,
but the Army had this one.
Could haul a lot,
even artillery.
Man, did that thing kick up a lot of wind,
blew away tents and everything else.
But it could hover,
and you could climb up a ladder into the back of it,
and we did.
And that's not counting
Puff the Magic Dragon,
the AC47 gunship that was adapted from C47 transport plane,
from the Big War,
and had guns coming out from everywhere,
making a lot of puffs.
And it's a pretty safe bet
that wasn't what Peter, Paul, or Mary had in mind.
Or even
Mark 47,
the official designation of napalm bombs.

Lots of stuff,
lots of puff.

Day 48: Another Patton

So there was this M48 Patton tank.
Shipped over there in 1969.
New, modern, fast.
Could fire HEAT rounds.
It had a few problems, though.
It had a thin underbelly,
which made it vulnerable to mines,
which the VC tended to use,
and there were concerns about ammo exploding inside
(which it did once),
and dust and humidity caused shorts and electrical failures,
(and where did we read something about dust and humidity?)
and ammo spillages and fire were a constant danger.
Oh, and the main gun failed a lot too.
Some way to honor a famous general.
Wonder what George would have thought of that,
(Patton, not C. Scott, although he might have had a few ideas).
It could fire guided missiles,
but they were never shipped over there.

Day 49: You say you want a ...?

Chinese sages believed that the Hexagrams
in the *I Ching*,
or Book of Changes,
contained the permutations and combinations
of all of life on earth.
Confucius regarded studying the hexagrams as studying life.
The lines change continually,

but they do so consistently,
so that someone studying them gradually comes to know them
and recognize how one event develops from an earlier one.
Questions put to the *I Ching* should not be too specific,
like, What should I play in the Exacta?
or with the magic 8 Ball: Am I going to get that date?
but more like
What will be the result if I continue the present course of action?
Anyway,
Hexagram 49 is about Ko,
Revolution.
So revolutionary change is called for,
or is coming on its own.
Now one may be reluctant to join in,
because a revolution is never trusted
until its results have been seen.
However,
placing oneself at the forefront of the change
can bring great success.
So then,
your aims will be furthered by your perseverance
and all regret will disappear.
Now, it seems that aims being furthered
and regret disappearing
would depend on which change coming about
that one has placed oneself on the forefront of
which.

Day 50: Aloha

What's the only state that is a legitimate R&R destination?
That's right, it's the 50th state.
Right out there in the Pacific.
Partway home.
Talk about so close and so far.

They use real money,
and they speak English,
no matter what they look like.
It's like being home,
if home has blue skies and water
and palm trees
and Diamond Head.
And when the smiling guy at the reception center says
"You don't have to build bunkers or do guard duty here,"
Some laugh
But others, sigh and think, Oh, good, that's a relief.

Day 51: Highway 51

U.S. Highway 51
Runs just about the length of the country,
Almost right in the middle.
"Highway 51" was a song Bob Dylan sang
on his debut album,
Bob Dylan,
in 1962.
Coming from
"Highway 51 Blues"
by Curtis Jones.
Talks about
"If I should die before my time should come,"
Which seems prophetic for a lot of people over the next decade.
Highway 51 even runs past Graceland,
making it something of an honored road.
Dylan will go on to sing about a lot more than Highway 51,
including spirited protest
of the war, among other things.

Day 52: Ground n air

It isn't always about battle.
Not that kind of battle, anyway.
Sometimes it's a battle to keep things normal, real.
And a deck of cards, 52 cards,
keeps it real, somehow.
Five at a time, or seven, or whatever it is.
You win money, you lose money.
Sometimes you don't even play for money.
It's something that feels like home.
Or it's something that feels nothing like home.
But holding those cards in your hand
looking at them
makes you feel like you have control
over something.
Over something.
Even if it's five cards
that just won't cooperate,
that won't be the five you need them to be.
It can be a battle with those cards,
but at least they aren't trying to shoot you.

So that's on the ground.
But up in the air
is the B-52,
aka Stratofortress.
It's a bomber.
And when it drops its bombs,
the ground shakes, for miles around.
It's terrifying even if
you're not where the bombs fall.
Someone once said a struggle will be won
not by those who can inflict the most
but by those who can endure the most.
If they can endure a B-52 bombing,

they can endure a lot.
And they did.

Day 53: Up there

When the Flying Banana started to look inadequate,
it was replaced with
the Sikorsky HH-3
"Jolly Green Giant"
combat search and rescue
(CSAR)
helicopter,
which was itself replaced by
the HH-53 "Super Jolly Green Giant."
So called because it was big
and green
and a welcome sight to ground troops.
It could provide firepower from the air
to support ground forces.
It flew into enemy territory to rescue downed pilots
and could hover for hours.
It was generally a fan favorite.

Day 54: And while we're hovering...

CH-54 Tarhe.
Named after a chief
of the Wyandot Indians.
also called the Skycrane.

I mean, you should have gotten a look at this thing.
                    It
              looked
Like the whole   middle was missing.

And it worked like a crane,
could pick up almost anything,
even another helicopter.
Looked weird up in the sky,
what with that   missing middle,
but it could haul a lot of stuff.

Day 55: 55 gallons

We got this thing called a 55-gallon drum.
What a history. It dates back
to World War II, WW2, the big one.
Carries 55 gallons of … something or other, usually something
    you can't drink.
Of course, exact capacity varies
with wall thickness and other factors.
Two holes, including a bung.
Who ever thought of that word?
These things, their size, shape and weight make them fit
four to a pallet, and they can be moved around
(did they plan it that way,
or did it just happen?)
on a two-hand truck,
provided you can get a side of the drum up enough
to slide the truck edge underneath it.
They can be cut
in a variety of shapes and sizes
for a variety of uses.
Like cutting one in half to burn stuff in.
But, now get this,
in England and Canada they call it
a 44-gallon drum,
because their gallons aren't like our gallons.
They use imperial gallons
Nothing imperial about us. Oh no.
We're a democracy. That's why we're here.

Day 56: Den been what?

The battle of Điên Biên Phu
lasted 56 days, including the surrender,
although some refer to it as a siege.
One day more than it took the South Vietnamese to lose Saigon.
One day for every signer
of our Declaration of Independence.
Fifty-six days for one battle?
That's like Joltin' Joe's hitting streak.
The battle of what?
I mean, who ever heard of Điên Biên Phu?
Other than some egghead with nothing better to do.
But you see, Điên Biên Phu was the French stronghold
that really wasn't so strong.
Because the French lost,
the French Union's Far East Expeditionary Force,
La (la?) Bataille de Dien Bien Phu, in 1954,
and thus the First Indochina War,
(isn't it a bad sign when wars can get numbers?)
and that meant France lost Vietnam,
thus ending its *mission civilisatrice.*
And that meant,
after the country was divided into two countries,
or only a temporary military division,
again,
that there was going to be continued conflict
over the future of those people
in those two countries.
And that meant
that other countries were going to get involved.
And who do you think that meant?
American paper writers please copy.
Because we didn't want to "lose" any more
countries to those Communists.
But Điên Biên Phu didn't have to fall.

It was not a foregone conclusion.
It took some doing by
a lot of people called Viet Minh
under the command of General Giap.
Vo Nguyen Giap.
He was a guy who learned from his mistakes.
A teacher and journalist,
who outlived them all,
and who said journalists weren't worth anything,
or teachers can't teach us anything?
He made mistakes two years earlier
against the French at Na San.
And picked up valuable lessons
that helped him a whole lot at Điên Biên Phu.
The French made a lot of mistakes too.
A lot of mistakes,
especially underestimating
those funny-looking little Asians.
Teacher Giap taught them lessons.
At Điên Biên Phu.
It was too late for the French to learn from their mistakes,
so they tried to help us learn
from their mistakes.
But we weren't listening.
We knew better.
We could do it better.
So much for French lessons.

Day 57: All the variety

Some days.
So what does Day 57 have for us?
Funny you should ask.
There's the M57. Check in tomorrow.
And Senator Joe McCarthy gave the Red Scare

a rousing kickoff when he said
57 employees of the departments of State and Defense
were communists or sympathizers.
(He later bumped it to 205, what with inflation and all.)
There was a 57 mm recoilless rifle.
And 57 percent of eligible males received draft deferments during
     the war.
In 1968 crimes of violence in the USA had increased 57 percent
     from 1960.
There was a B-57 Canberra bomber.
Ordinance 57 was a land-reform program in South Vietnam.
Bob Hope (who you'll remember from Day 9)
made 57 trips total in his life.
In December of 1968,
the U.S. Supreme Court refused to review
the federal government's right to send reservists to Vietnam
in the absence of an official declaration of war.
This was from an appeal
by 57 military reservists.
Talk about variety.

Day 58: Pounding feet

Yesterday we had the M57.
It was also known as the clacker.
Today we have Jozsef Misznay and Hubert Schardin.
Today we have Norman MacLeod,
naming the new anti-personnel mine
after a Scottish weapon.
The claymore, the M-18A1 claymore.
Utilizes the Misznay-Schardin effect
to be extremely lethal,
requiring 58 foot-pounds to deliver its load.
Effective to about 110 yards,
although it can go as far as 270 yards.

Day 59: Just once to the lake

It was 59 colleges
represented
at Lakeport, Michigan,
in June of 1962
to issue what came to be called
the Port Huron Statement,
the statement of the SDS
Students for a Democratic Society.
It would call for
an effort to end racism,
an effort to be supported
by the Democratic party,
and,
mindful of the Cold War,
not arms control,
but
universal,
controlled
disarmament.
Rejected Communism (saying the movement failed).
It even got something
from Day 261.
'Twas an effort
that had as much success
as our armed effort
in Southeast Asia.
And funny thing is,
in both cases,
people started out with the best of intentions.

Day 60: M60

In AIT they taught us how to fire an M60 machine gun.
Like this: Fire burst of six.

But when you really open it up, it can go much farther: much.
Deadly.
More than 500 rounds per minute at its highest rate.
And the barrel gets so hot it has to be changed
or it will droop,
and not from the saltpeter.
Could it really do that, like in a cartoon?
In AIT we did night firing, with tracer bullets
that we could watch going through the night sky
like thousands of furious lasers,
thrilling to watch, in a way,
and scary knowing how death-dealing they could be.
It can be fired off a tripod,
but in the jungle it worked best on its own bipod legs.
It wouldn't be too easy to set up a tripod
and mount the M60 on it,
if a firefight broke out.
It was the GMPG—the General Purpose Machine Gun.
We just called it the machine gun, or the M60.
The medal citations would say,
"He dashed through an intense hail of enemy machine gun fire."
Couldn't have been very intense
if someone could dash through it
and live to collect a medal.
Must not have been an M60, I guess.

Day 61: They Marched Into Sunlight

From far away
Came the news
The old unit
The original unit
The one I started with
But was transferred from
Marched into sunlight

And sixty-one of them
Never marched back out.
Boots on the ground.
Boots in the air.
Boots never found.
Boots anywhere.

On a rotation, Alpha, Bravo, Charlie, Delta,
And Headquarters, always Headquarters.
That day it was A and D
And Headquarters.
I had been in B, Bravo. One that stayed behind that day.
The one the guys I knew were in.
A major catastrophe.
And a colonel catastrophe,
and sergeant and spec/4 and everything else.
And a general embarrassment.
"After you go Phuoc Vinh, many GI die,"
I hear in Lai Khe
I nod.
Not the first thing I want to hear on a visit
to the old stomping grounds,
Hoping her shop would be a refuge, an escape
(her younger sister liked me).
I mean, I already know, but
it's tough to deny when somebody who saw it
tells me about it.
Bodies were lined up along the road,
Or so they said.
They said,
"I've never been so scared in my life."
"It was awful."
"They were using first aid packs over again."
"It only took two choppers to bring back all the guys
Who weren't killed or wounded that day."
How many to take them out, maybe twenty-five?

Back at battalion,
Guys were being asked to ID the bodies.
Like in a crime show.

People get killed in war, yeah.
But what the fuck happened?

Day 62: Battle tested

Bringing in the big guns.
On September 30, 1968.
The Battleship New Jersey.
BB-62.
"Big J"
could fire a shell 23 miles
out of its 16-inch guns.
Most decorated battleship in US Navy history,
with 19 battle stars.
Won the Navy Unit commendation "for exceptionally meritorious
     service."
Engaged in gunfire support missions,
south of the DMZ.

Day 63: Hunkering down

There was this memo.
It was sent to Robert McNamara,
the Secretary of Defense,
saying that 63 percent of the enemy infantry targets
we encountered
were personnel in trenches or bunkers.
This meant
that the enemy could control
the rate of combat losses

by determining when to initiate combat.
It went on further to say
that increased US troop strength
would not significantly affect
the attrition rate
of enemy forces.
So one might wonder,
why,
knowing that,
we kept increasing troop strength.
Just hunkering down
into what we knew, maybe?

Day 64: Just missing it

Lyndon Johnson,
LBJ,
was 64 when he died,
in 1972,
a week before the ceasefire
that ended the American role
in the war
associated with him.
He tried to win the war
on his own,
an unwinnable war,
just as he tried to win
the war on poverty.
Also unwinnable?
He kept thinking he could make it happen.
Just as he had made so many things happen.
But it never worked out that way.
And the war over there
took many of the same people
who the war on poverty

was meant to help.
So they never got to live
in the Great Society.
Nor did he, really.
RIP.

Day 65: Your money's worth

In addition to regular pay,
and overseas pay,
there was hostile fire pay.
$65 a month.
Not bad money in those days.
Not that it was much of a compensation.
But at least somebody realized
that it wasn't just another tour of duty.
That's something.
Isn't it?

Day 66: Not getting any kicks

1967 wasn't such a quiet year.
A total of 66 people
died in the rioting that summer.
43 in Detroit.
23 in Newark.
That's not counting Watts two years earlier,
or Hough one year earlier,
or what would happen the next year.
More (much) to come on that year.

Day 67: The way the trends are tending

We tend to think of political preferences
as political parties,
in the USA,
when we tend to think at all,
but they couldn't exactly come up with parties
in Vietnam.
In 1964, the best they could do
was identify 67 "political tendencies"
in South Vietnam.
The only real "party" anyone could identify
was the NLF,
the National Liberation Front.
But that was the party of the guys up north,
(We sort of knew them as the Viet Cong),
the party we were trying to cause to crash.
That's the trouble with a party:
Deciding who to invite.

Day 68: The year that was

And if you think 1967 was loud,
let us not forget
the late, great
1968.
Now that was a year.
The Year of the Monkey.
"The Year of the Barricade."
The year of
hair-raising
Hair.
The year of
The Days of Rage.
A year

of days of rage.
And not just in the USofA.
Students in France,
joined by millions of wildcat strikers,
making the government look shaky,
and
Prague Spring,
Warsaw,
and
guerrilla warfare against the military dictatorship of Brazil,
the Tlatelolco Massacre
in Mexico.
The hits just keep on comin'.
The year started, pretty much,
with the Tet Offensive.
A victory that was a loss,
or a loss that was a victory.
Depends on one's perspective, I guess.
Who was it who said
"Another such victory, and I'm done for"?
The battle for Hue
set its own "standards"
for savagery
as the struggle for liberation
raged.
And that's not counting Mini-Tet,
the second-wave offensive:
119 towns shelled,
154 American KIA,
and 326 South Vietnamese.

1968 ended, pretty much,
with 16,899Americans dead
(the single-year record,
for those of you who keep track of such things)
and

with a presidential election.
But in between…
in between.
Before reaching the Promised Land,
a Dreamer died.
As did a younger brother who became the oldest brother,
for a short while,
and campaigned as anti-war,
as did a McCarthy, but not Joe.
Black Panthers were roaring.
And
there were those national conventions,
one of which tried to mimic
the violence going on
across the globe.
Or maybe even surpass it.
Kind of drew attention away from
what some were trying to draw attention to.
But Nixon was the One
who won.
This one.
And the year goes on.

Day 69: Life's a beach

Sun, sand, surfin' —
There were a lot of guys
who couldn't wait to return to that.
For them, the Beach Boys sang about
The things that mattered.
Even guys who weren't exactly surfers
Thought of home
When they heard the songs.
They had an album,
Beach Boys 69.

Yeah, it was released in 1981,
and in London,
of all the surfing places,
but still,
they had their fun, fun, fun.

Day 70: Ground meat

The frustrating thing about fighting a guerrilla war
is that the guerrillas don't stand and fight
the way you want them to.
Except sometimes they do.
Like in the Au Shau Valley,
in May of 1969.
The name of the place
was Dong Ap Bia,
or Ap Bia Mountain,
but our guys called it Hamburger Hill,
maybe because they felt as though
they had gone through a meat grinder.
Because the North Vietnamese
decided to take a stand,
a stand that lasted ten days,
ten of the longest days
in the lives of many,
and the end of the lives of 70 GIs
(although not everyone agrees on that number).
The 101st Airborne,
the Screamin' Eagles,
and ARVN units
went uphill,
fighting to take a hill
that the enemy fought to keep,
until the enemy abandoned it,
slipping away during the night.

After they lost 630,
we think.
It caused a lot of questioning,
about tactics
and about the war itself.
even in the Senate.
Oh, and when it was all over,
we abandoned it too.
It had no tactical or strategic significance.

Day 71: Pointing the way

In 1956,
there was NSC 5612/1,
which was a
statement of policy on U.S. Policy
(from the Department of Redundancy Department)
in Mainland Southeast Asia.
It had
71 points.
And those 71 points included
a Supplementary Statement of Policy
(somebody must have really liked the word policy)
on the Special Situation in North Vietnam.
It called for a rollback policy (what, did someone get a bonus
    every time the word was used?)
toward North Vietnam,
aimed at reunification of the country
under anti-Communist leadership.
71 points,
and they didn't lead to anywhere.
And,
the official number
of shows on *The Smothers Brothers Comedy Hour*
(Not counting "Pat Paulsen for President"—

a *sui generis* if ever there was one)
was
71.
Coincidence?
You be the judge.

Day 72: M72

The M72 is called a LAW:
A Light Antitank Weapon.
Sometimes even called a Log.
It is meant to destroy tanks.
At least that's what it was designed for.
Part metal, part plastic,
with a carrying strap, it folded up to about two feet long.
Fires a rocket
to an effective range of 300 meters.
To arm it, pull out the pin,
grasp the half-ring, and pull it out to its full length.
It even has a picture of a soldier holding one
one the side of it,
kind of like a toy.
But it's no toy; it has
a back-blast just like a regular bazooka,
like the one that obliterated an orange crate
way back in AIT.
Except that the VC didn't come at us too often with tanks.
So we used it as a bunker-buster.
If we found a bunker.
Or something else to shoot at,
like a headstone.

Day 73: Think 73

James Brown,
The Godfather of Soul,

Soul Brother Number One.
He sang a song "Think"
And then sang it again in 1973, calling it "Think 73."
Asking her to think about the things he did
and the things he didn't do.
He did give black America
someone to look up to
and feel a pride in,
even asking them to say it loud.
He asked his brothers and sisters
not to burn after Martin Luther King was killed,
but rather to give their kids a chance to learn.
He went big time and still kept touch
with those on the street.
In Nam or at home,
they listened to him.
Could he shake up a stage.
Think 73 was an interesting new version?
It was also his age when he died.

Day 74: The City of Light

The Paris Peace talks.
They were the talks that were going to end the war,
and leave everyone deliriously happy,
like the opening of the League of Nations 50 years earlier
that was going to end all war.
Well, they might have been delirious,
because the Paris Peace Accords
had 74 different articles,
under nine chapters and three protocols, of course.
Who could remember them?
Doesn't matter,
Because no one abided by them anyhow.
But we loved Paris in the springtime,

and in 1968
and in 1969
and in 1970
and in 1971
and in 1972
and in 1973.

Day 75: Real women

There were women we did meet, though.
The nurses, in the military,
who worked to help the wounded guys heal,
and the Red Cross women
and the USO women
and any other women
who were over to help us,
mapmakers, decoders, air traffic controllers, photographers,
    translators, even clerks in base hdq.
They were real.
They had clothes on.
They tried to keep our spirits up
back at the base camps,
but they didn't stay in the base camps.
Some of them even came out to visit us
in places like the Iron Triangle,
where guys had been killed.
And they came out there
without helmets
or weapons
or any of the equipment we carried.
Real women,
who smiled at us
and talked to us.
God damn!
Now that took guts.

And they did it just to make us feel better.
Did they get medals for that?

And out of all that,
75 women,
and a baby girl,
died over there.
8 military,
(including Sharon Lane,
who merits her own Day, 312)
67 civilian.
Not with a weapon,
or a grenade,
not storming a bunker,
or on patrol,
but trying to bring help,
or comfort.
And that's just on our side.

How many women died
in all of the war?
A good guess:
We don't really want to know.

Day 76: The Big Parade

Okay, we got 76 trombones that led the big parade,
with 110 cornets right behind.
Rows and rows
of the finest virtuosos.
Horns of every shape and kind.
50 mounted cannon.
Copper-bottom tympani in horse platoons.
Double bell euphoniums and big bassoons.
And clarinets of every size.

So that's
76 trombones,
110 cornets,
50 mounted cannon,
a whole load of virtuosos,
horns,
tympani,
horse platoons,
euphoniums, big bassoons,
and clarinets,
and one big parade
more
than will be waiting at the end of this year.

Seventy-six.

It ain't just trombones, though.
No sir.
Did you know that's the percent
of Nam vets
who came from lower- or middle-
or working- class families?
That's a lot of class,
lower- or middle- or working- .
Seventy-six.
That's the spirit.

Day 77: Phu Two?

The siege of Khe Sanh
lasted 77 days,
in early 1968,
although operations there ran longer.
It was a gallant stand by our Marines
dramatized nightly

on the TV news.
Westmoreland
was looking to stage a big battle,
and thought Khe Sanh was the place.
So when the enemy attacked Saigon
during the Tet offensive,
Westy thought the Saigon attack
was meant to draw our attention
away from Khe Sanh.
Actually,
It was the other way around.
But that wasn't the only mistake
we made in that war.
And to get really scary,
we contemplated using nukes
around Khe Sanh.
And some people wondered
how it could have gotten any worse.
That's how.

Day 78: Have a future?

We got another type of cards.
Tarot.
A deck of 78.
Not so easy to fill a flush maybe,
but great stuff for looking into the future.
For example, there's Card number 13
(how lucky can you get?),
and it's Death.
But Death isn't about death.
No?
No, it's about lasting change
(couldn't death be lasting change?),
dramatic, profound, or radical.

The decision has been made,
and the course of the change cannot be altered.
It will usher in something new.
Yeah, well, like I said…
Then we got the fives.
The middle arcana, they're called.
Now they're something.
They represent change, challenge, or fluctuation.
Like the five of cups,
which represents deep sorrow,
the loss of something that cannot be recovered.
That don't sound too good.
Or the five of swords.
Yeah, now that sounds like a good one.
Uh, well.
It represents self-defense,
although it can stand for the conqueror or the conquered.
Then there's the five of pentacles.
That's a lack of support, a breakdown of belief systems,
     or the effects of bad choices.
And the five of wands, representing
stiff competition, fair or otherwise.
Who knew?
It was in the cards, man.

Day 79: M79

M79. It's a funny-looking thing.
Kind of short and stubby,
with what looks like a pipe as a barrel.
It's called a grenade launcher.
Because it launches a grenade.
The grenade is smaller than the ones we wear on our belts,
and throw if we need to.
But it fires, launches, them a lot farther: 300 yards.

Three fucking football fields?
So they tell us.
Frag, and even smoke, 40 millimeters.
They even tried a plastic stock
because the wooden one could get swollen.
But you have to be careful when you fire it.
You can't put your thumb behind that locking lever
or you'll get hurt.
So keep your thumb to the side
when you fire a grenade.
But you don't have to worry about that
on Day 203.

Day 80: Missing, but not by as much

Ho Chi Minh died,
eight months before he turned 80,
and six years before
his efforts bore fruit,
and he got a city named after him.
That victory came
thirty years after
he declared
a democratic republic
of Vietnam.
He started the declaration by saying
"All men are created equal.
The Creator has given us
certain inviolable rights:
the right to life,
the right to be free,
and the right to achieve happiness."
It was written with the help
of people of the OSS.
That was the original

CIA.
Yeah, we worked with him
during World War II.
Funny what war does.

Day 81: 81 millimeters

The heavy weapons infantry,
those 11C and 11H guys,
they fire mortars,
81 millimeter.
Heavier lugging
than what 11B guys had.
But a whole lot of damage
when they landed.
Maximum firing range was a 45 degree angle.
When they yelled "Short!"
You knew you were in trouble
because it could land anywhere.
It was one weapon
that both Joe and Nguyen used.

But then it turns out
that the VC used an 82 millimeter mortar,
so they could fire our rounds but we couldn't fire theirs.
A silly millimeter wider.
What more will they think of?

Day 82: Morale problems

And they weren't caused by yesterday's mortar situation.
The constant drafting
and replacement of troops
was a problem, so they said.

The lowering of standards
would lead to trouble,
so they said.
Maybe they were right this time,
because in 1968
the Army reported
82 convictions for mutiny
or
refusal to follow orders.
Given a never-ending war
that seemed to lack any purpose
that wasn't so surprising,
was it?

Meanwhile,
back at home,
the Joint Chiefs of Staff
reported that
the 82nd Airborne Division,
the All American Division,
holding down the fort at Fort Bragg,
was the only readily deployable army division
still based in the U.S.,
all the others
being deployed
outside the U.S.

Day 83: What is in a name anyhow?

Supposedly,
there were 83 named operations during the war.
Who does the naming anyway?
(And who keeps count of how many there were?)
That must be a great job.
How do you get one?

Is there a special course you have to take
at some secret military location
with drill instructors?
"No, no, you don't hold the pen that way!"
"You can't give an operation a name like that!
Get your head out of your ass!"
And then can someone come along
and say they don't like the name?
What do you do then?

Day 84: Muggy with a chance of misery

The annual humidity of Vietnam
averages 84 percent.
To the GI humping the boonies,
lugging ammo, canteens, maybe a backpack,
not to mention extras,
like claymores and LAWs,
and of course a weapon,
and all topped off with a steel pot,
that sounds like low-balling.
I can break out into a soaking sweat
just standing in one place.
Eighty-four?
And that's Fahrenheit?
Not kilometers or decagrams or something?
You sure it isn't a hundred eighty-four?

Day 85: Enlightenment

Regardless of what system is in place,
Vietnam has a strong Buddhist tradition.
So strong
that South Vietnam had a population

that was more than 85 percent Buddhist.
But Ngo Dinh Diem,
the guy we were keeping in power (for a while),
he wasn't.
Buddhist, that is.
In fact, he even tried to suppress Buddhism.
Tried to suppress a religion
held dear by more than 85 percent of the people.
And this was the guy we were propping up
as boss of South Vietnam,
why?
Well, because he didn't like Communism either.
Was he popular?
Well, depends on who you ask.
Take 1955, for example.
He arranged a vote on who would be head of state.
He won, with 98 percent of the vote in South Vietnam.
And you think that's good?
In the Saigon area,
out of 450,000 registered voters,
he got 605,025 votes.
That's right,
he won 133 percent of the vote.
I mean, Ho Chi Minh could only pull down
about 90 percent each election.
But 133 percent.
That's a percentage
any politician would envy.
No wonder we kept backing him,
and giving him a lot of money,
which he readily accepted.
But there were quite a few people who didn't like him,
like Thich Quang Duc,
a Buddhist monk who set himself on fire,
immolated himself, as we like to say,
in a form of protest

that 65 others would follow.
It probably was not the way
Gautama had in mind, and
unfortunately,
it led to no enlightenment in this country.
Because in the fall of 1963,
Diem was overthrown (not to mention shot and killed)
in a coup we somehow thought
would make things better, for us.
Ngo Dinh Diem was gone,
as was his brother,
but the problems remained.
Or got worse.

Day 86: WHAM

Page 86
of the "Pacification Program" handbook
refers to
Winning Hearts and Minds,
WHAM,
of the Vietnamese people.
Yes, well
we WHAM'd them pretty good,
didn't we?
On more days
than this one.

Day 87: Tuned in

In 1966,
just to pick one year,
87 percent of Americans 18 and older
watched television.

This was good news to the television stations,
but not so much to many government officials
when they saw that what many Americans were watching
turned out to be images of our boys
getting killed and wounded,
muddied and bloodied and bandaged
and needing to be medevac'd
in a war that would not end—
"The Living Room War"
as it came to be known.
And the funny (???) thing is,
the TV stations weren't trying
to criticize the war.
They were trying to show what heroes
our fighting lads were.
But somehow,
something
didn't look so heroic.
(Real soldiers didn't look quite as good
in mud and blood and sweat and bandages
as John Wayne did.)
Of course, that's when they weren't showing campus
    demonstrations
that the newspapers were so in tune with
that they sent their crime reporters to cover them.
And LBJ wondered why there had to be television news at all.
He should have been around in 2003.
Stay tuned.

Day 88: The widening gulf

In the 88th Congress assembled
88 Senators approved
a joint resolution,
The Joint Resolution to Promote the Maintenance of International

Peace and Security in Southeast Asia,
(that led to a lot of joints
being smoked, if not resolved)
or just
The Gulf of Tonkin Resolution, or
the Southeast Asia Resolution, or
"Asia Resolution, Public Law 88-408."
That law, passed in 1964,
gave the president unlimited power
to conduct the war
(that wasn't a war)
as he saw fit.
And things weren't the same after that.
But two senators
voted against the resolution
(ten weren't around that day).
Morse
(who predicted that those who voted Yes would regret it)
and Gruening.
Must have been the Pacific Northwest atmosphere.
They both lost when they ran again
(refer again to that Day 68 thing).
At the junction
of bad voting and bad timing.

But there was another junction.
At the junction.
Junction 88 was not some crossroad in Nam.
It was a movie with Pigmeat,
who got a lot of guys through that war
with "Hello Bill" and
"Kalamazoo 442" and
"Here's a dollar." "ONE dollar?"
and who they were really talking about when they said,
"Here comes the Judge."
And who, when he heard "Order in the court"

and said "Two cans of beer!"
was ordering for more than just himself.

Day 89: Toe power

89 was the total of goals scored
in the World Cup in 1962,
and the same again in 1966.
That was in 32 games,
down from 126 goals
in 35 games
in 1958.
It went up to 95 goals in 1970,
and 97, in 38 games,
in 1974.
We in the USofA
weren't too concerned about soccer,
or fútbol,
then.
We had more important things to worry about.

Day 90: Kill ratio. Six dead from Ohio

In any war,
there's them as gives
and them
as doesn't give.
Beallsville,
a town in Ohio,
gave.
Six guys from Beallsville died in the war.
Six?
Doesn't sound like much.
Except,

the population of Beallsville
was less than 500 (that's a 5 with two 0s after it).
Making it one (that's 1) out of every ninety (that's 90) residents
dying in that war.
Oh, the national average?
That was one out of every six thousand (that's a 6 with three 0s
after it).

Day 91: UCMJ

Article 91
of the Uniform Code of Military Justice,
the UCMJ,
covers insubordinate conduct toward
warrant officers, noncommissioned officers, and petty officers.
So it prohibits
striking or assaulting
warrant officers, noncommissioned officers, or petty officers
in the commission of their duty,
or
willfully disobeying
warrant officers, noncommissioned officers, or petty officers,
or
treating with contempt or being disrespectful in language or
    deportment to
warrant officers, noncommissioned officers, or petty officers,
and says that anyone who does any of those things
to
warrant officers, noncommissioned officers, or petty officers
will be punished as a court-martial directs.
The article
wasn't invented for the Nam,
but it got a real workout there.

Day 92: The Brooklyn Navy Yard

A lot of different guys
have a lot of different memories
of the Yard.
The place that played such a big part
in the futures of many people
From the New York Metro area.
Today,
Building 92
is the only building open to the public.
It has a museum, a job center, and even a café.
The Yard was closed as an active Navy yard
in 1966,
but it kept going for a long time
doing one thing or another,
staying alive
in our hearts and minds.

Day 93: Oil's well

The net profits of the world's largest oil companies increased
93 percent during the first half of 1974.
Just thought you'd want to know that
while you're looking for a gas station that's open.

Day 94: Welcome home

Actually, there was a group that was cheered
upon returning home.
In July of 1969,
94 soldiers were cheered
at McChord Air Force Base
when they returned home.

Ninety-four. So?
So, they were the first troops brought home
under the new troop reduction plans.
So, were people cheering them
or the fact that troop reductions were starting?
Who knows?
Does it matter?

Day 95: There's protest, and there's...

In 1517,
Martin Luther
nailed his 95 theses
to the door of a church in Wittenberg (that's in Germany).
That was his form of protest,
a protest that grew,
quite a bit.
Somehow one wonders
if nailing protests against the Vietnam war
to the doors of churches
would have had the same effect
as sit-ins, angry confrontations,
and even civilized discussions
(and I hear tell
there really was such a thing
once upon a time).

Day 96: Staying hydrated

Humping the boonies,
we couldn't have done it without canteens,
either metal plastic.
One quart of water,
That's 32 ounces per canteen,

So if you carry three of them,
Which most guys did by the end,
that was 96 ounces of water.
96 ounces of life,
96 ounces of something that felt
like a break of any kind
from the humping
and the heat
and the sweat.

Day 97: Weekend warriors, coastal guardians

The irony.
97 members of the National Guard were killed in Nam.
Didn't they join to avoid going over there?
They did,
but the need was becoming so great
that even a few Weekend Warriors
were sent there and got to take part,
although LBJ mightily resisted
large-scale activation.
You think that's weird,
seven members of the Coast Guard were KIA.
The Coast Guard?
Yes, this war gave everyone a chance.

Day 98: Growth spurts

Here's a tidbit
for you horticulturists.
Bamboo,
that stuff that's yellow when it's dry,
is green when it's alive.

It's a grass,
believe it or not.
and the largest timber bamboo can reach
98 feet in length,
and be more than 6 inches in diameter.
and in 24 hours,
it can grow 39 inches.
(It's that rhizome-dependent system, of course.)
More than a yard in one day.
Maybe that's why it provides such thick cover,
especially from aircraft,
in those triple-canopy areas
and is such a bitch to get through.

Day 99: Beneath the surface

A crew of 99 lost at sea
when the nuclear submarine Scorpion,
SSN 589,
was lost in the Atlantic,
on its way home.
Sailors, seamen, nowhere near the land war.
That happened in late May of 1968.
No one knows why,
although many theories have surfaced.
And that came five years
after the Thresher,
SSN 593,
was lost off the Massachusetts coast.
That sub had a crew of 112,
and
17 civilian technicians
who were there to observe.
Bad luck, bad timing, bad days all around.
How is it

that so many things happen
to take people's lives?

Day 100: 100 names

Legend has it
that there are 100 Vietnamese surnames.
That's because
Lac Long Quân,
the father of the Vietnamese people,
married Âu Co',
which makes her the mother of the Vietnamese people, I guess.
And Âu Co' gave birth
to a sac containing
100 eggs,
thus giving birth to 100 children,
all boys, no less.
And that was the origin
of 100 Vietnamese family names.
But Lac Long Quân (means Dragon Lord of Lac)
told Âu Co' that he was from dragons
but she was from fairies,
so they could not stay together.
They were as incompatible as
fire and water
or Mars and Venus.
They split up,
and they divided the kids between them,
50 each.
And Lac Long Quân went south to the sea,
and Âu Co' went north to the mountains.
Their son,
Hùng Vu'o'ng,
went north with his mother
and installed himself as the first monarch.

And all this was in 2839 B.C.
That's a long time,
to not be able to make it work out.

Day 101: The Eagles have landed

The 101st Airborne,
the Screamin' Eagles,
who will have other days this year,
were called into Little Rock, Arkansas,
when President Dwight Eisenhower,
exercising his authority as
Commander-in-Chief
of all American military forces,
sent them
to help those black students
enter Little Rock's Central High School
in 1957.
This was after Orval Faubus,
governor of Arkansas,
ordered reservists into town
to keep the black kids out.
It was also after Louis Armstrong
took a stand in favor of desegregation
in Little Rock
and criticized Ike strongly.
Satchmo also wore
a Star of David
because of things he saw in his life.
So the Screamin' Eagles were there to help assure
truth, justice, and the American way.
What a wonderful world.

Day 102: Uphill fight

There was this hill (more like a knoll really)
called Hill 102.
And in 1969
a chopper was shot down near there.
And an infantry company from the Americal Division
was sent to rescue the crew.
But they refused to go.
Must be more of that morale thing.
Anyway, eventually they did go,
and they found the crew,
all eight of them,
all dead.
None of the infantry were killed,
and none of them were charged either.

Day 103: 103 degrees

103 degrees is hot outside,
but even hotter inside a human. It gets close to fatal.
And that's how hot a temperature can run
with malaria,
thanks to those never-ending mosquitoes.
Hot, tired, weak, almost unable to move,
not thinking too clearly,
one guy passing out while walking across an airstrip,
just dropping while he's walking,
wearing all the equipment he'd need to go out on an operation.
When he comes back, cured, he says,
"The last thing I remember was walking out onto the airstrip,
and then the next thing I knew I woke up
and somebody was packing ice around my balls."
That'll wake him up.
That was to cool him down,

because his temperature
was around 103 degrees.

They handed out tablets to prevent malaria.
Chloroquine primaquine.
They usually worked,
except every once in a while they didn't.
And they could have the effect of loosening the bowels,
once in a while.

Day 104: Starfighter

There was a jet,
the F104,
called the Starfighter.
It was a single-engine,
high-performance,
interceptor aircraft.
It wasn't used in aerial combat,
but it was considered successful
in deterring MiGs.
It was fast
and could climb well,
but it had a bad overall safety record.
For example,
back in the world,
Maj. Robert H. Lawrence Jr.
was killed in a crash
of an F104
while on a training flight.
He was America's first
black astronaut,
and almost certainly would have flown on a space shuttle.

Day 105: Ground n air, again

On the ground was the 105 mm howitzer,
A lightweight towed cannon.
It did a good job supporting the infantry.
Keeping those artillerymen busy,
during firefights,
or even at night.
Fire for effect.
In the air was the F105 Thunderchief,
the jet plane capable of delivering nukes
on the Soviets,
if we ever decided to do that.
But here it was used to hit targets
up there in North Vietnam.
It flew more combat missions over North Vietnam
than any other Air Force craft.
No nukes,
just lots of bombs
that did a lot of damage.

Day 106: Elementary

You think there was no progress anywhere?
Well, when this war started
There were 100 known elements.
But by the time it ended,
there were 106.
Those six new guys were synthetic though.
I thought only …
Never mind.
Four of them were radioactive.
Talk about nuclear proliferation.
But don't worry,
because number 2,

Nobelium,
or No,
forms a stable divalent ion in solution.
Phewf.
So if they can synthesize six new elements,
why can't they make a ham and lima beans C-ration that doesn't
    taste like shit?

Day 107: The Norwegian sense of humor

From 1955
(the unofficial date of the start of the war)
until 1975
(the official etc., etc.),
107 Nobel Prizes were awarded.
Peace prizes were not given every year,
but they were given in 1973
to Henry Kissinger and Le Duc Tho,
for their part
in the Paris peace talks,
surprising a lot of people,
including Henry Kissinger and Le Duc Tho.
Kissinger didn't attend the ceremony,
and he donated his share of the money
to children of service members
killed or missing.
Le Duc Tho wouldn't even accept the award,
saying he'd wait
until peace was truly established
in Vietnam,
thus helping to prove
that the North Vietnamese
were extremely patient.
And he was at Loc Nonh in 1975
to oversee the final offensive drive

that established peace
eventually.

Day 108: Eastern canon, not to be confused with western cannon

The Upanishads,
the end of the Veda.
The meaning goes back to sitting next to a teacher
or having a connection between them.
There are more than 200,
of which the Muktika contains
108 canonical Upanishads.
They offer insights
on being,
or real identity,
or sense of self.
The image of two birds in a tree,
the lower one,
in a state of anxiety,
is the individual ego.
The higher one is free of fear
and sees itself in relation to other things in the world.
this seeing enables it to become them
and thus expand its consciousness.
Hell,
in our country,
we got drugs that can do that.

Day 109: Hot winter

109 veterans
and 16 civilians
gathered in Detroit

from January 31st to February 2nd, 1971.
Sponsored by the Vietnam Veterans Against the War,
the Winter Soldier Investigation
brought together people who wanted to show
a relationship between military policy
and war crimes.
By talking about atrocities
they witnessed or even committed,
they hoped to challenge both
the morality
and the conduct of the war.
Did it do any good?
You're kidding, right?

Day 110: 110 from the Frozen North

From north of the border,
our border, 54-40,
without a fight,
as some of us who didn't want to fight
went north,
some of them came south,
and they were sent southeast
to fight
in our war.
110 Canadians died in Nam.
That's the official number anyway.
Did they wander south and get drafted?
Did they believe in it enough to join us?
Or did they just want to live in the U.S.,
and that was the price they had to pay?
Looks like we'll never know.
110 KIA.
And that's not counting the 7 MIA.
What happened to them?
Eh?
Oh, Canada.

Day 111: Aardvark

The F-111 was a new plane,
a swing-wing plane,
an all-weather, low-altitude
fighter-bomber,
called the Aardvark.
Both the Navy and Air Force liked it,
although their ideas varied a tad.
Both services got it,
with slight variations.
It got to Nam in 1967,
when it promptly proved to be a loser.
It was improved eventually, however,
so that it was able to fly missions successfully at the very end.

Day 112: How hot was it?

I'm dreaming of a quick getaway.

Third Country Nationals.
TCN.
That was the term our folks used in Saigon
for anyone who wasn't American or Vietnamese.
As the end approached
and became increasingly obvious,
TCNs were given instructions
on evacuation.
They were told to get a move on,
to un-ass that area,
when they heard the following over Armed Forces Radio:
"The temperature in Saigon is 112 degrees and rising."
This would be followed by the playing of
"I'm Dreaming of a White Christmas."

Day 113: APC

An M113 was an armored personnel carrier.
Or an APC.
It's armored, and it carries personnel.
And shovels, and water, and ammunition
and who knows what else.
And it carries guys wearing flak jackets,
sometimes with no shirts.
Talk about sweaty.
The front and back are pretty heavy,
even if the sides are kind of light.
It can get a little stuffy.
But it beats walking, beating the boonies,
on the days we're lucky enough to get a ride.
"Second of the Second went mechanized."
The 2nd battalion, 2nd infantry (regiment, for those who must
      know).
They ride every day.
Lucky fuckers.

Day 114: 114

One that didn't last:

The M113 was such a success
that they came out with the M114.
Supposedly an armored recon vehicle,
it was supposed to be a lighter version of an APC.
Didn't work out so well.
It had mechanical problems,
it didn't have much oomph,
and it fared worse than an M113
when it hit a land mine.
It was scrapped.

And one that did:

A newspaper strike in New York
that lasted 114 days
in 1963
led to
the founding of the
New York Review of Books.
So even if readers in New York couldn't get
their daily report
of the war that hadn't started yet,
they could get something
far more valuable,
and enduring,
hard as that might be to believe.

Day 115: Market Time

When we realized we needed to patrol water
instead of just land,
Task Force 115 (originally Task Force 71)
was formed as a Coastal Surveillance Force,
to patrol waters that were too shallow
for big ships.
It was under the Naval Advisory Group.
It was called Operation Market Time.
And, since it involved coastal patrol,
Coast Guard cutters were called in.
They had a reputation for seaworthiness.
But
this meant
a more operational role,
other than just an advisory one
for the USA.

Day 116: Game Warden

So now we have coastal patrol,
but now we need river patrol,
because in the Mekong Delta area,
there is not much road traffic
(because there aren't that many roads)
and a lot of river traffic,
because they's a lot of rivers.
And that means
Task Force 116,
and Operation Game Warden.
It used the Patrol Boat, River,
or PBR,
which could go very fast,
powered by water-jet pumps.
They came from the Jacuzzi Brothers.
Doesn't that make you feel better already?

Day 117: MRF

And then there was
Task Force 117,
the Navy's Mobile Riverine Force
or MRF.
This was a joint Army-Navy task force
organized for combat operations
in the Mekong Delta.
It meant the Navy's resources could move the Army's infantry
fast,
like 240 kilometers in 24 hours.
It used different craft,
including updated Monitors,
that looked a whole lot more fearsome than the original.
and it worked pretty well,

although terminology sometimes caused problems.
But see what happens when we work together?

Day 118: Raindrops keep fallin', and fallin' ...

The annual rainfall can vary,
but the high end
is 118.1 inches.
That's in a year,
not in a day,
although it sure as hell felt like
the daily rainfall during the rainy season,
which could also vary.
But hey,
they need all that rain to grow rice.
and we've got to at least let them have that.
And that's something you can think on
while you watch the rain drip
off the front of your helmet.

Day 119: Full accounting

We wanted all our boys brought home.
So when there were reports
of 119 reported sightings
of Americans held in Vietnam against their will,
the Joint Task Force-Full Accounting (JTF-FA)
investigated.
None of the reports proved true.

Day 120: Making the weight

The minimum weight
to be eligible for the draft
was 120 pounds.
Believe it or not,
some guys
(maybe the ones who couldn't get under 31 on the written)
were able to starve themselves
to get under the weight,
and thus be rejected.
And they weren't jockeys.
That takes a lot of dedication.
It sounds like the cutting edge
of America's weight obsession.
And all it took was a war.

Day 121: EC 121

The Air Force and Navy both had an EC121.
The Warning Star.
It was an early warning aircraft
used a lot in Vietnam
and other places.
It studied radio signals.
On April 15, 1969,
the North Koreans shot down
an EC121 Constellation
that was flying over the Sea of Japan.
Only the North Koreans said it was flying over their waters.
The entire crew of 31 was killed.
It was a routine Beggar Shadow
intelligence-gathering mission.
We sent a fleet to the area
and announced we would continue our

intelligence flights
as before.
This was a little more than a year
after they seized the Pueblo,
claiming it had violated their waters.
We got the crew back,
except for the one crewman killed,
but they kept the ship.

Farce, war, frenzy, torpor, slavery! Day by day those sacred doctrines of yours will be wiped out, whenever you conceive them and admit them untested by natural philosophy.

Marcus Aurelius, *Meditations*

Day 122: Hands-on teaching

1965 was a big year
for Teach-Ins around the country.
Questioning the war
and maybe more than that.
Originally they offered
a pro-war and an anti-war speaker
a chance to present their cases.
The first Teach-In was
organized by the SDS, and held
at the University of Michigan.
They started by talking about the draft
(military induction, not bad insulation)
and ended by talking about
how to take over the campus.
That went over so well,
they had another one two months later
at Cal Berkeley.
Jerry Rubin was prominent.
That went over so well
that by the end of the year
there were 122 Teach-Ins around the country.

Day 123: Dangerous cargo

The C123 was a cargo plane.
It saw quite a bit of use.
In 1962,
JFK authorized
an aerial defoliation program
using C123s
to drop Agent Orange.
Pamphlets were dropped later
telling people the chemicals were harmless.

That was being economical with the truth,
especially as Operation Ranch Hand
expanded after 1965.
They could also carry human cargo,
such as the one that crashed into a mountain
in December of 1965,
killing four American crewmen
and 81 ARVN soldiers.

Day 124: Another one of these

Then there was NSC 124,
a draft statement of U.S. policy,
in the early 1950s,
on U.S.-Vietnam relations.
It warned of the possibility
of China being willing
to send troops into Indochina,
even Thailand or Burma.
The objective of NSC 124 was
"to prevent the countries of Southeast Asia
from passing into the Communist orbit."
The Joint Chiefs weighed in,
warning that this would mean
an increased commitment in many areas,
but
the Joint Chiefs concurred with the recommendation.
They also opposed a French withdrawal from Indochina
because they thought that would mean
the USA would have to move in to take over.
They nailed that one at least.

Day 125: The day you get it and the day you get rid of it

At the end of 1970,
We gave the South Vietnamese navy
125 vessels from the U.S. Navy,
thus ending our role in inland waterway combat.
This brought the total of vessels turned over
to 650.
This was part of Vietnamization, but
17,000 Americans would remain
with the South Vietnamese navy
in shore positions
and as advisers on vessels.

Day 126: In the saddle

In case you need this when you get home,
126 pounds is the weight colts carry in the Kentucky Derby
(although fillies can carry 121).
So there are jockeys
who weigh less than
126 pounds,
or even less than 120,
because they can add weight on the saddle.
Probably didn't matter what the weight was
for Secretariat.
In 1973 he won the Triple Crown,
with the first sub-two-minute Derby,
then the Preakness,
and then the Belmont by 31 lengths.
He was back in the stall chowing down on a bucket of oats
or filling a bottle
by the time the last of them crossed the finish line.
Or maybe, because it was New York,
he wanted to beat the rush hour.

Day 127: Underground, man

The Viet Cong
were able to do well, in part,
because they were able to live underground.
For example, tunnel complexes
in the Iron Triangle
(yeah that place, of which more will be heard)
and Cu Chi
totaled about 127 miles.
To give you some perspective,
that's just shy of the distance
from Washington, D.C.,
to Philadelphia.
Some of these places had four levels,
with barracks,
hospitals,
recreation areas.
Some way to live.
But they did it.
And today,
those Cu Chi tunnels
are a tourist attraction.
There might be a lot of attractions in Viet Nam
I'd be willing to tour,
but that ain't one of 'em.

Day 128: More WHAM

128 VC.
That was the official version
of the body count after we went into My Lai.
That was a slight underestimation,
especially because we liked high body counts, didn't we?
Well, let's go for it then.

Give credit where it's due.
The Peers Investigation estimated
that the dead numbered
(doesn't that sound like they're doing something active?)
between 175 and 200
"VC" including children, women, and old people.
Even that might be too modest.
An investigation by the CID showed 347 civilians dead.
And those news reporters,
well, we know what we think about them,
but anyway,
they estimated between 450 and 500.

Day 129: Military justice

129 courts-martial
(doesn't that plural sound like they really mean business?)
after the LBJ prison riot.
This is one event that was kept pretty quiet.
For one thing, a lot of the rioters were black—
because a lot of the prisoners were black—
so it looked like a race riot,
and that wasn't the kind of thing
we wanted the folks at home to hear about.
After all, things at home were bad enough.
We also didn't want the folks at home
to be reminded that we needed a stockade
to confine our brave young fighting men
who weren't conducting themselves in a military manner,
or that there were so many of them
(as you'll see on Day 140)
that conditions were deplorable,
thus maybe causing the riot.

Day 130: C130

Even grunts get to fly once in a while.
In a C130 airplane.
The C130 Hercules.
Big. I mean BIG.
Four engines.
"Their top speed is classified information," someone said.
They can carry troops,
they can carry supplies,
they can even accompany B 52s on a bombing run.
And some of them were converted to gunships,
making them AC130.They can load lots of us inside
to get us somewhere in a hurry.
No stewardesses, no meals, no movies.
You get on, you go there, you get off.
We sit on the floor.
Takeoffs and landings
can be kind of sharp,
so it won't be too easy for the enemy
to take a shot at this big thing.
And when someone did take a shot,
the landing became a quick, steep un-landing.
So quick and steep that one guy, a new guy,
got sick.
He puked into a sandbag,
filling it with something other than sand.
That was after he asked me for my helmet.
What was he thinking, anyway?

Day 131: Maximum maltitude

131 degrees.
What's that, the temperature when we were out on patrol
    yesterday?

No, that's the temperature reached
in the malting process for beer.
Whoa, you got my attention already.
I thought I would.
Do you want that temperature in centigrade?
Will it help me get the beer any faster?
No.
Then just give me the beer.

Day 132: Full blast

The maximum range of a flamethrower,
was 132 feet,
although the effective range
was about 65½ feet,
with a rate of fire
of half a gallon per second.
That's napalm,
but if that doesn't sound impressive,
watching the flames come out of it
was very impressive.
Maybe terrifying would be better.
It weighed 68 pounds full,
but to the guys carrying one,
it felt more like 680 pounds.

Day 133: Listen

The U.S. Civil Rights Commission
issued a report in 1967.
"A Time to Listen ... A Time to Act"
that urged the American people
to make the deterioration of our cities' slums
a national priority.

It was 133 pages long,
including endnotes.
Ah well.
Guess we had a lot on our minds.

Day 134: Death reaches out again

The U.S.S. Forrestal,
one of our carriers,
was used to send jets
to bomb Vietnam.
On July 29, 1967,
134 crewmen on the Forrestal died
in a fire and explosions,
when, in a freak accident,
a rocket fired across the flight deck.
It took more lives
than any other single naval incident.
Some died when they had to jump.
It has been said
that John McCain
was able to get out of his plane,
which was on the flight deck,
just in time.
Saved from death
for something worse?

Day 135: Stratolifter

There was a C-135 transport plane,
the Stratolifter,
with a cruising speed of 530 mph and a range of 4,000 miles,
but a small load capacity.
There was also a KC-135 Stratotanker,

an airborne refueler,
and a KC-135A.
A little story about them.
In 1966,
a K135 and a B52 collided
over the Spanish Mediterranean coast.
There were nuclear bombs on board.
None of them exploded, although
there was some radioactive release.
One went underwater and was recovered
three months later.
It took 100 divers,
a bathyscaphe,
and two miniature subs to get it.

Day 136: Dead end streets

Dear Raymond,

Your mother has asked me to write to you
because she is too grief-stricken.
Your cousin Joshua
was shot and killed yesterday.
Apparently,
he was involved in an altercation
with a man named Rashad,
whom I think you will recall
as Marvis Simmons
from the neighborhood.
It happened on 136th Street,
although it could have been
on any street in this country
that has nothing but a dead end.
I hope you will accept
my most sincere condolences.

My heart is ravaged
by yet another death
of one young black man
killed by another.
Must it take a gun
for our voices to be heard?
I feel at a loss.
Although I wish the best for you
I must admit that I oppose the war
that has put you in such danger.
And yet when people your age
come seeking my counsel
I don't know what to tell them.
Should I encourage them to stay home,
refuse to serve a country
that treats them so shamefully,
all the while knowing they might well be shot and killed
right here at home?
As a man of God,
I know I should not say this,
but sometimes I despair. I despair.
I pray every night for guidance.
I try to follow the example of Doctor King,
and speak out for what I believe,
but I'm not always sure what to believe.
Please know that I pray also for your safe return.
Your mother tells me
you intend to continue your education.
I am pleased to hear this,
and I am sure you will excel.
If you find the time to write back to me,
would you share your thoughts?
I know it might be presumptuous of me,
someone who could never even undertake
the burdensome duties you perform every day,
to ask you to take the time to write,

but I would value your opinions.
At any rate,
I look forward to your homecoming,
and God grant that we have an opportunity
to sit down and talk one day.

Yours in God's love,

Pastor Adolphus Jackson

Day 137: Reaching out

Operation Outreach.
137 centers
assisted veterans.
The centers were opened
as a result of Operation Outreach,
a counseling program
funded by Congress,
at the instigation of
the Vietnam Veterans of America.
It was funded in 1983.
It takes Congress a while to get going on these things.
So about ten years
after they came home,
counseling was available.
Sort of like the aggressive job placement,
that was available to the Vietnam veteran
who wanted a job as a janitor.
But if he was looking for something more ambitious,
executive, say,
then it wasn't so aggressive.
But it was good enough for government work.

Day 138: Maybe it's perspective

In November of 1966,
138 prominent Americans
signed a document,
"A Crucial Turning Point in Vietnam"
that criticized critics of war policy
for failing to make
"the distinction between responsible dissent
and unfounded attacks on our society."
Further,
it urged
"men of stature in the intellectual, religious and public service
      communities"
to withdraw their support of the fantasies of
extreme critics of the Johnson administration.

Day 139: Wrong way, Kilroy

In March of 1970,
the U.S. announced a new method
for measuring the progress of our pacification programs.
District advisers would answer
139 "more or less" objective questions.
A computer would interpret the information
gleaned from the responses
and give a scorecard.
And the results?
Well, in the first month of this new method,
the number of hamlets
relatively pacified
went from 92.7 percent
to 89.9 percent.
That's "more or less"
not the direction we hoped to be going.

Day 140: Different accommodations

The original stockade
at Pershing Field
at the air base
in Tan Son Nhut
was meant to hold 140 prisoners.
When it got to
more than 200,
they moved the whole thing
to Long Binh,
making it Long Binh Jail,
yet another LBJ.
Even that got overcrowded,
with 14 prisoners in tents
meant to hold 8.

Day 141: Lifting the stars

The C141 Starlifter.
It was an airplane
That had a cruising speed of
495 miles per hour
and a maximum range of 6,140 miles.
By mid-1968,
14 squadrons were in service.
It could do a lot,
and one of the things it did
was to bring POWs
from Hanoi to the Philippines
on their way home.

And that leads us to

Day 142: Home at last

The first batch of released POWs
was 142,
sent off very low-key
from Hanoi's Gialam Airport.
More to follow.

Day 143: "Engine 143"

From the tradition of American train wreck songs,
and eventually
the Carter family,
came "Engine 143"
a song about a brave engineer
who died in a crash
because he wanted to stay with his engine
in West Virginia
in 1890.
Supposedly it was the last song
Johnny Cash recorded in its entirety.
Joan Baez sang a version of it too.

Day 144: Marching, but not exactly in step

144 is the approximate number
of antiwar groups
that marched on Washington
in mid-October of 1965.
So there were people working at it early
to keep you from being sent there.

Day 145: Down

The United States lost
145 fixed wing aircraft,

just in 1971.
For what it's worth (or "For What It's Worth"),
that's one craft
for each minute
of the Academy Awards show
the previous year.

Day 146: Same old song

Long after the French left Vietnam,
1970, to be exact,
146 young people were killed
in a dance hall fire in Saint-Laurent-du-Pont,
in France,
near Grenoble.
The victims were aged 17-25.
Investigations would find
six serious safety violations,
and 806 buildings would be closed down
throughout France.

Day 147: RPV

A remotely piloted vehicle,
or RPV,
had a 147 designation.
It could be used in several ways.
The 147-SC, for example,
was the most commonly used in Vietnam,
flying more than 1,600 missions at low altitude,
doing reconnaissance.
The 147-NA was sent on radar-jamming missions.
The 147-J, the first daytime low-altitude recon RPV
in Vietnam, was used over North Vietnam

below the heavy overcast of the rainy season.
Those planes could also be used
to fly decoy missions or drop leaflets.
Too bad we couldn't find more ways to use equipment
that had no humans in it.

Day 148: Extra credit

In the Spring of 1968
(that year again)
148 students were arrested
in a protest at Columbia University.
They took it to the streets
to protest the war, yes,
but they also protested the university's plan
to construct a new gym
in an area that would require relocation
of black people living in nearby apartments.
But
the gym would have a "back door"
for the local population,
a door meant to cope
with the altitude difference
of Morningside Heights
(or White Harlem, to George Carlin)
although it was not interpreted that way.
The demonstrations also brought out
differences between black and white students,
protesting for different reasons.
Plans for the gym were scrapped
and a different one was built.
The war went on.

Day 149: Welcome to the world

In 1977,
well after our shooting had stopped,
Vietnam,
the one country, not North and/or South
would join the United Nations,
along with Djibouti.
This brought UN membership
to 149.
President Carter
gave his approval,
after Vietnam released
more information on MIAs.

Day 150: Flech and blood

Up to 150 yards,
a beehive round can kill anything
within a path 50 yards wide.
That's the XM546, 105 mm beehive,
containing 8,000 flechettes.
They're little things like arrows or darts,
that leave the artillery barrel
in a projectile.
Then a fuse detonates the base charge,
blasting off the forward shell,
and releasing those flechettes.
Called beehive because
they make a buzzing noise when traveling.
Can be deadly,
deadly,
especially when fired in an open area,
like the length of an airstrip.

Day 151: The MUTT with a pedigree

Officially,
it was the M151
Military Utility Tactical Truck.
Unofficially, the MUTT.
A lot of people just called it a jeep.
Either way,
it got around, a lot,
and did a lot of work,
a lot of driving.
Officially,
it was first put into service in Vietnam,
meaning it,
like many American GIs,
got a real baptism by fire,
learning about war and the military
in a hurry.

Day 152: Ya seen one war...

The television show
Combat! —
with a bayonet for the exclamation point, no less—
ran for 152 episodes,
from 1962-67,
making it the longest-running TV drama
about World War II.
(Started in black and white, ended in color.)
Irony here,
in that Robert Altman directed some of the episodes,
and then went on to direct the movie
*M*A*S*H.*
And if that's not enough,
Vic Morrow,

Sgt. Saunders in *Combat!*,
would be killed while filming a Vietnam segment
in *Twilight Zone: The Movie*,
in 1982.
And more Twilight Zone to come.

Day 153: There's that light at the end

In 1969,
U.S. command in Saigon
announced American KIA
at 153,
for the week ending July 5.
It was the lowest casualty figure
in six months.
So should we be happy
or not?

Day 154: The Bard

Shakespeare
(you might remember him from high school,
unless that was when you were out grabbing a smoke)
wrote 154 sonnets.
Numbered, conveniently for us,
from 1 to 154.
Of those, the first 126 are to a fair youth.
And it would seem that some of the lines
from those sonnets
are pertinent for this war.
Like this one from Sonnet 15:
"To change your day of youth to sullied night."
Alas, the day of youth became sullied night
and not much else

for many young Americans
in this year.
Or this from number 19:
"Oh, carve not with thy hours my love's fair brow,
Nor draw no lines there with thine antique pen."
For more than 58,000,
No antique pen would ever draw lines
on a youthful brow.
And from number 9:
"The world will be thy widow and still weep
That thou no form of thee hast left behind."
And there were a whole lot of them
who left no form of themselves
once they were gone.

Day 155: Even louder

In addition to the 105 mm howitzer
was the 155mm howitzer.
Big.
And LOUD.
There was the M109,
which was self-propelled,
and the M114A1,
which was towed.
It got a lot of use
in this war.
It could send a round a long way away,
supposedly 16,600 meters.
And did we mention it was loud?

Day 156: Re-cycle, re-use

The iron triangle
nowadays refers
to congressional committees,

the bureaucracy,
and interest groups.
But back then,
the Iron Triangle meant
an area in which the VC
had a near iron grip.
From about
Ben Suc
to Ben Cat
to Phu Cong,
or thereabouts.
In February of 1967,
in order to take the iron out of it,
our decision-makers sketched out
a 156-square kilometer free-fire zone,
and in Operation Cedar Falls
the area was
bombed,
shelled,
napalmed,
and bulldozed
(or Rome plowed if you prefer),
to get rid of a tunnel system
of about 125 miles.
It worked at the time,
capturing many supplies.
But,
those tunnels?
Maybe those bombs and shells and bulldozers
and that napalm
missed something.
Because the tunnels were used again,
as staging grounds
for the Tet offensive.

You know, it's funny,

but the original *Twilight Zone*
supposedly was 156 episodes.
Somehow that seems fitting,
but I can't quite put my finger on just how.

Day 157: 500 miles

In 1971,
Al Unser
(he wasn't known as Sr. then)
won the Indianapolis 500,
with an average speed of 157.735 miles an hour.
It was the second year in a row he won.
And this second time
was on his birthday,
May 29, believe it or not.
And believe this or not,
he would go on to win it twice more,
in 1978 and 1987.

Day 158: From our house to your house

We sent a lot of planes
over North Vietnam,
and the North Vietnamese shot a lot of planes down.
How'd they do it?
Well, partly with
158 SAMs,
as in surface to air missiles,
not Uncle,
that the USSR donated
to North Vietnam.

Day 159: More girl power

Believe it or not,
there was still a Women's Army Corps,
the WACs,
during this war.
Their peak strength
In Vietnam
was 159,
including enlisted personnel and officers.
This was in January of 1970.
They were also in Japan
to accommodate
the needs of hospitals.
They didn't get the "opportunity"
to die in combat,
as their later sisters would.

Day 160: Open door

160 U.S. marshals
were injured
in the fall of 1962
when James Meredith
tried to enter the University of Mississippi
as a student.
Two people died.
Looks like some people
weren't too happy about the whole thing.
The U.S. Army was there too.
And a general's car was set on fire.
Some things never change.

Day 161: Kiwi power

Just so you know
the USA wasn't going it alone,
way back in 1965
New Zealand sent
the 161st Battery of the Royal New Zealand Artillery,
its first combat troops,
to Vietnam in 1965
(on our side).
The Battery's mission was
to support Australian forces.
New Zealand would maintain troop strength
at same level from 1967-69.
It began to withdraw troops in 1970,
and withdrew them all in 1971.

Day 162: Extra effort

In 1972,
Just in time for Valentine's Day,
American fighter-bombers
flew 162 strikes
on infiltration routes and bases
west of Kontum,
especially their Base Area 609.
It was one of the heaviest bombing raids
of the war,
up to then, at least.
Wound up not doing much good, though,
because a month and a half later,
the North Vietnamese launched
the Nguyen Hue Offensive,
which (very) eventually led
to North Vietnam's victory,

even though in May
we bombed the daylights out of them even more,
even into the North.

Day 163: Talk about a gut course

The Marines had
A 163-hour course of instruction
At the Marine Corps Cold Weather Training Center.
It was about
evasion, escape, and survival.
It was meant to show
what it was like to be a POW.
163 hours.
That's some course.

Day 164: How much is that in croissants?

In 1950,
Congress
(the U.S. Congress)
authorized $164 million
(that's USA $)
for arms, ammunition, aircraft, ships, tanks, trucks, and jeeps
to help the French
with their war effort in Indochina.
After all, what are friends for?
But if that sounds like a lot of money
for something made in France,
check Day 342.

Day 165: GI Bill

The Servicemen's Readjustment Act.
Better known as

The GI Bill.
Because everyone else gets the meal
and the GI gets the bill?
Nah, it was just a name for a law.
Anyway, in 1969,
the payout was
raised to $165 a month,
for full-time students.
$165 a month with which
to pay tuition,
buy books,
eat,
get to campus
or live there
and go wild
with any other expenses.
It was less than
WW2 veterans got,
but hey,
we learned from that
not to go giving those guys too much help.

Day 166: Yo Rinnie

The Adventures of Rin Tin Tin
ran for 166 episodes.
from October of 1954 to May of 1959.
The GI of the Sixties
got to watch
those hardy, intrepid cavalrymen
and Rusty "B Company"
and of course
Private Rin Tin Tin.
And who could forget the episode
about the White Buffalo?

'Cause you'll only find him
if your heart is brave and true.
Yes,
holding down Fort Apache
and keeping the West safe
for those white settlers
who were trying to bring civilization
to a place needing civilization.
Soldiers defending democracy
against the savage hordes.
Sort of like ...
Oh, never mind.
Maybe we should have taken a closer look at *F Troop*.

Day 167: A lousy deal

Classics Illustrated,
that series that put
some of the world's best literature
into comic book form,
folded with its 167th issue
in 1962.
It was *Faust*.
Classics Illustrated started
with *The Three Musketeers*
in 1941,
and sales
had been 25 million,
a week,
in the 1950s,
but they fell beneath the onslaught
of television,
and mass volume paperback books.
Yeah, the (very) abridged and illustrated form
lost out to the book form.
Go figure.

Day 168: Loyalty oofs.

Data collected,
in Operation Mission (USOM),
of loyalties
showed that
in 1965,
out of 12,537 hamlets in South Vietnam,
168 were controlled by the government.
Talk about not even hitting your own weight.
Ouch.

Day 169: Taking it to the streets

In the week after
that heavy day,
April 4, 1968,
169 cities
reported racial violence.
46 people were killed.
Or 47, counting the day itself.

Day 170: Health and well-being

The Agency for International Development
or AID,
part of the State Department,
was the principle U.S. agency
for design and implementation
of U.S. nonmilitary development
and assistance.
Anyway,
it helped build at least 170
district maternity dispensaries.

But balancing that, maybe,
a North Vietnamese document says
the U.S. bombed 170
hospitals, sanatoriums, infirmaries, and pharmacies,
just from February 7, 1965
to June 30, 1966.
So it kind of evens out.

Day 171: Rolling Thunder

171 U.S. aircraft
were lost in Operation Rolling Thunder.
That's out of 55,000 sorties,
and 33,000 tons of bombs dropped.
That was to prevent North Vietnam
from arming
and equipping
their troops in the South.
Except,
from all available evidence,
it had almost no effect on them.

Day 172: Olympian heights

172 events
in the Summer Olympics
in the elevated elevation
of Mexico City,
which stood out
above sea level, 7,300 feet
(or 2,200 meters, as scored by the East German judge).
The USA stood out
with 107 medals,
45 gold, 28 silver, 34 bronze.

And Tommie Smith and John Carlos stood out,
maybe not as much for how
they won their gold and bronze medals
as for how they accepted them.
And Aussie Peter Norman stood
between and with them.
Their stand on the stand
and the spirit of the times
went hand in glove,
as it were.
That got a lot of people's attention.
They went faster.
And Dick Fosbury stood out
for succeeding
when he flopped.
He went higher.
And Bob Beamon stood out
with a world record
when he went farther.
and his record went farther
than records usually go.
And Debbie Meyer became
the first American woman
to splash her way to three individual golds.
She went faster, wetter too.
And stronger?
American Joe Dube lifted
550 kilos,
which is a hell of a lot in any language.
And that was only good for a bronze.
A bronze?
And do we even need to say what year all this was?

Day 173: All the way

So, the 173rd Airborne Brigade
makes the only large combat jump
in this war; 2nd Battalion did the jump.
in Operation Junction City,
(see Day 282)
to cut off enemy escape routes.
Parachutes in the sky
as men jump out of airplanes.
Landing in different terrain
from what they practiced on.
Maybe we'll scare the enemy
wondering what is flying down on top of them.
Unless they're not there
to be flown down upon.
Here they go.
All the way.
Our paratroopers showed their stuff,
but the enemy didn't show anything,
holding fire then,
as always,
until the time that suited them best.
Fighting their kind of war
all the way.

Day 174: Woody Sez what?

Woodrow Wilson "Woody" Guthrie
wrote 174 columns
under the heading of "Woody Sez"
and appearing in *People's World*
in 1939.
Sort of Woody's observations
on life,
in a variety of ways.

Woody was
sort of a Communist,
and sort of not.
He did care about
everyday people though.
He inspired
a great many musicians who came after him,
including some who would sing out
against the war,
like Pete Seeger,
and Woody's son Arlo,
who had his own adventures
with American life.

Day 175: The best and the barracuda-est

In 1965,
175 students at Harvard Law School
sent telegrams to the White House
in support
of LBJ's war policies.
So there.
I mean,
they must have known, right?
They were the smartest cats in the room.

Day 176: Happy are those...

176 is the number
of verses in the longest chapter in the Bible (just about any),
that is, Psalm 119 (or 118 if you're Greek).
In the Hebrew Bible,
it has 22 verses,
one for each letter of the Hebrew alphabet.

This offers the Torah as the source
of blessing and right conduct.
Even the Christians view it
as something David used
to teach Solomon
not only the alphabet
but also
the rules of life.

Day 177: XM177

All right,
so you didn't like the M16
just because it didn't work.
Well now there's
the XM177,
the modified version of the M16.
It has a collapsible stock
and a different flash suppressor.
It fires the same ammunition,
more effectively than the M16, it seems.
Looks real impressive too.

Day 178: Petits Canadas

Cher Enfant,
I hope you are doing well, coping with the weather
and everything else.
We are doing well here.
Hockey season will be starting again soon.
It seems to me that it just ended.
So of course your father and grandfather
can continue their arguments.
Dad says your grandfather
should stop rooting for the Canadiens now

because we are Americans
and have been for a long time.
Your grandfather says
he is still a Petit Canada,
and that means he's still Canadian.
Dad says the "petit" means he's
not Canadian any more
and should root for the Bruins.
Grandpa laughs and tells Dad
how many Stanley Cups
the Canadiens have won
and asks how many the Bruins have won.
I guess it isn't very many,
but you know I have never tried to keep up.
That reminds me about Petits Canadas.
your sister was looking up something about them
in the library,
and she said that in 1927 there were
178 Petit Canada doctors,
just in Massachusetts.
So you see,
we don't all work in the mills.
To be honest, I never would have thought
there would be that many back then,
but there were.
Please take care of yourself.
I'll be glad when you are back here
so you can join the arguments.
I looked at your Bruins banner today.
Your Dad says they'll win a Cup soon,
and he'll get you a brand new banner,
and even a real shirt.

But don't tell him I called it a shirt,
I still can't think of it as a sweater.
I'm still praying for you.

Write when you can.

Love,

Maman

Day 179: Read alla 'bout it

The war must have been of interest
to somebody back home.
There were
179 American correspondents
covering the war in 1968—
and that's just the American ones.
There were 114 from South Vietnam—
well I guess that's not so surprising—
and 171 from other countries.
That's a lot of reporting.
179 American correspondents.
One for every U.S. helicopter that will be lost in 1972.

Day 180: Double time, march

You probably weren't aware of this,
and probably didn't care if you did,
but double time
means
180 steps
per minute.
So get a move on.

Day 181: Crying time

In 1963 and 1964,

the army gathered
about 181 tons of
powder to make CS gas.
That was a form of tear gas.
It was used sparingly at first,
but more later on,
although it was probably used
more at home
than anywhere else.

Day 182: All aboard

The National Railroad Passenger Corporation,
better known as Amtrak,
began business in 1972.
It wasn't exactly public
and not exactly private.
Anyway,
it started with 182 trains.
That might sound like a lot of trains,
and then again it might not,
but it would represent
a cut in passenger service
of about 50 percent
from previous private operations.
But still,
somebody was making the trains run,
on time?

Day 183: Long gone

B.B. King
got to 183
on the *Billboard* all-time Top 500
with his version of the
Roy Hawkins and Rick Darnell song,

"The Thrill is Gone."
Yeah, I guess by the time
B.B. King's version came out,
in 1969,
the thrill was gone for a whole lot of people.
And we're past the halfway mark.

Day 184: Interrupted flight

The U.S. Air Force
would lose 184 colonels
in the war.
And that's not counting lieutenant colonels.
That's just full colonels,
bird colonels,
who probably would have been familiar
with Day 207.

Day 185: To a T

Now make sure you get this right
When you're cooking over that lump of C-4.
When water just starts to bubble
It is about 185 degrees.
That is the right temperature for oolong tea.
And then steep
For two to three minutes.
Now make sure you do it right.
Civilization is depending on this.

Day 186: Unaffiliated

In 1973,
CBS had 186 affiliates
around the country.
But

in August of that year,
94 of them,
just more than half,
refused to run the drama
Sticks and Bones,
a Tony winner
about a blind Vietnam vet
and his bitter homecoming.
It ran 100 minutes,
and some of the stations that did run it
ran it without commercials.

Day 187: Circulating

Circular Telegram 187
of Nov. 27, 1950
contains the text of a press conference
by Dean Rusk,
who was then Assistant Secretary of State for Far Eastern Affairs.
At the time, he was concerned about Korea,
its relations with Japan after the war,
and the North-South division
in that country.
The Korean War
and the encroachment of Communism
were important factors
throughout his life
and would play a part
in his views on Vietnam

Day 188: MIL-STD 188

MIL-STD 188
is a set
of military standards

relating to telecommunications,
made necessary when the Department of Defense
was unhappy with technical deficiencies
in telecommunications systems and equipment.
It started out as a document
for tactical and long-haul communications,
but eventually applied
to tactical communications only.

Day 189: Project 100,000

Although LBJ will forever be linked
to the Vietnam War
(go figure)
he also wanted to build the
Great Society.
Ironic then
that so many of the people
he wanted to help
were sent to his war.
Anyway,
one program of the Great Society
was designed to extend the social and economic benefits
of military service
to disadvantaged or underqualified Americans
by boosting their education and job skills,
because a report showed that 600,000 men
failed the Armed Forces Qualification Test (AFQT)
each year.
So,
out of 134,000 participants,
or 354,000, depending how you look at it,
who were put in government-backed referral programs,
189 received any viable training.

Day 190: Taking stock

Charlotte Motor Speedway,
the home base of the stock car racing community,
is really located in Concord,
but heck,
we're not going to quibble.
It's a mile-and-a-half track,
that regularly sees lap speeds of 190 mph.
Shoo-ee.
Hosted its first race in 1960.
Them stock cars
gave Richard Petty a way to make a name for himself.
27 victories
in NASCAR Winston Cup races in 1967.
By the time he retires,
that 27 will be a single-season record,
as will his 200 career victories,
as will his 10 in a row.
Started in a Plymouth,
finished in a Dodge.
Just wanted to race cars.

Day 191: Still with the Tar Heels

State Route 191.
It's an original state highway,
Running from about Hendersonville to Asheville.
Long about 1966,
While this here war was going on,
plans were started
that eventually would make it
part of what would become
Interstate 240.
That part of the interstate system

is now known as Billy Graham Freeway,
named for
the Pastor to Presidents
and a native Tar Heel.

Day 192: Hill 192

There was an incident
at a place called Hill 192
in November of 1966.
Only one Vietnamese was killed,
so it didn't matter.
Did it?

Day 193 Swift boats

They were called Patrol Craft, Fast,
but they were better known as Swift Boats.
193 of them were built,
although not all of them were used.
They were originally intended for coastal patrol,
but they did inland work as well.
They were fast, hence the name,
and reliable and sturdy.
They had a .50 cal. machine gun
and mortar combination
that was quite effective.

Day 194: So rare and true

"Peggy Sue"
by Buddy Holly
ranked 194
on the *Rolling Stone* 500 greatest hits of all time.

Day 195: Sort of like "The Lottery"?

In order to be equitable,
yeah,
they set up the draft lottery.
That meant that for the draft,
someone picked a day of the year
and then picked a number,
so the day and the number
would be linked
and the first guys called
would be the ones born on the days
starting at 1.
The number they needed to call
went higher in some places
than in others.
but in 1970,
the number went as high
as 195.
The following year,
as we "Vietnamized" the war,
it only got as high as 125 or so.

Day 196: Turn out the lights

The 196th Light Infantry Brigade
was raised in Fort Devens, Mass.
It arrived in Vietnam in August of 1966,
so, pretty early then,
and it went through several permutations.
It was the last American combat brigade
to leave the country.

Day 197: State of the art

In 1975,
in other words around the time
our involvement is over,
a Smith-Corona portable electric typewriter
goes for $197.
Maybe GIs can benefit from a program
that teaches how to service them.
That is sure to serve everyone
well
into the future.

Day 198: MSC Peacock

MSC 198
was the USS Peacock, a coastal minesweeper.
It could sweep moored or bottom mines,
and it came from Japan
to take part in Operation Market Time,
as well as other overseas assignments.

Day 199: Getting in on the ground floor

The 199th Light Infantry Brigade
arrived in Vietnam in December of 1966.
So it too was there pretty early.
It sustained
more than 3,200 casualties
from then until the fall of 1970,
before being deactivated at Fort Benning.

Day 200: Peace, love, understanding, and hospitality

In 1973,
North Vietnam
had 200 representatives in Saigon,
a military delegation,
to supervise the peace.
This was part of an agreement
of the Paris Peace Talks,
as the USA tried to disengage,
and the war slouched
toward an end.
The representatives
even gave a press conference
every Saturday morning.
Wonder if they rode around
in a Lambretta 200.
Or even a 550.
And how many Lambrettas would it take
to carry all those representatives around,
five, six?
American representatives would have needed
a lot more than that.

Day 201: Not that they'll ever offer to let you see it

A 201 File
is a complete history
of any individual
who serves in the military.
Imagine what some of the entries are
from the Vietnam era.

Day 202: Tanks for the proletariat

Believe it or not,
North Vietnam had tanks,
although we didn't see many
and didn't give much thought to them.
They don't often play a prominent part
in a guerrilla war.
But the 202nd Tank Brigade,
of the People's Army of Vietnam,
or PAVN,
or North Vietnamese army, as we thought of them,
did exist.
It was formed in 1959.
It played a big part
in the final push to victory.

Day 203: The new grenade launcher

One day the sergeant says,
"You're the grenadier. Here."
And he hands him this thing.
"What the fuck is this?"
He says, "It's an M16."
"It's not an M16," he says.
"All right. It's an M203. It's the new grenade launcher."
"Grenade launcher? It's an M16
with some kind of tube underneath it."
"Yeah. That's the grenade launcher."
Replaces the XM148.
Looks like a joke.
"That's so in addition to carrying a grenade launcher,
you don't need to have a .45 as a sidearm;
you can use the M16."
"Will it work?"

"Don't know. Guess we'll find out when the time comes."
Actually, what he said was,
"Yeah, it'll work. It'll work fine if you take care of it."
What he thought was,
"Don't know. Guess we'll find out when the time comes."
"Yeah, great. Hey, wait a minute. Does this mean
I have to carry grenades and M16 ammo both?"
"Yup."
"As if I don't have enough shit to carry."
"Hey, life's tough in the Asian Theater of Operations."

Day 204 Viva la différance

204 people at Cambridge University
voted against giving an honorary doctorate
to Jacques Derrida
(scholar, from France by way of Algeria).
Didn't matter,
since 336 voted in favor of giving it to him.
Derrida's essay "The Ends of Man"
appeared in *Philosophy and Phenomenological Research*,
taking a stand against the Vietnam war (ours, not France's).
But if you think he caused a stir with that,
get a load of Deconstruction.
Sacre bleu!

Day 205: Reading the signals

The first signals regiment
of the PAVN
(the North Vietnamese, aka the guys we were fighting)
was the 205th Signals Regiment,
although it was originally the 303rd.
It could trace its origins to 1945.

One of its missions
was to maintain a station
for radio communication with its people
in South Vietnam.
It did that pretty well, it would seem.

Day 206: Turning point: Another thousand
or so

206.
Remember that number.
Because that's how many thousand
additional troops were requested
just for Vietnam,
on Feb. 28, 1968.
206,000.
That's additional troops.
Additional to the 525,000 or so
there already.
And that's important because
sending that many more troops
would mean
not only continuing high draft rates
but also
activating 262,000 reservists,
with the possibility they could be sent over there.
It would also raise costs,
which already were high,
and casualty counts
even more.
The country would be
on a war footing
(see: USA, December 1941 to August 1945).
And those numbers,
206,000

and 262,000,
made LBJ
and everyone else
stop and think about the whole thing,
even hawks in Congress
(some of them anyway).
And
the other side of that consideration
was that if we didn't send those
206,000
additional troops,
that was tantamount
to conceding
that we couldn't win the war.
LBJ asked Clark Clifford to conduct
an "A to Z" review of the situation.

And the result of that Alpha to Omega review,
short version,
was that we couldn't win there
and were making a mistake by trying.
So, see what a difference
206 could make?

Day 207: Wild blue yonder

West Point and Annapolis
went way back,
but after World War II,
the USA set up
the United States Air Force.
And if there was going to be an Air Force,
there needed to be an Air Force Academy
to turn out the officers who would be needed
for the new Air Force.

The first graduating class,
in 1959,
had 207 graduates.
And
where was the first place
those graduates
got to show their stuff
in a combat situation?
That's right.

Day 208: The creation

The Vietnamese people,
North, South, or uncommitted,
usually consider their history to have begun
in 208 BC.
That's when
a rebel Chinese warlord by the name of Trieu Da
declared himself ruler of a large area,
calling it Nam Viet.
The country would go through a lot
since then.

Day 209: Fragmentary information

There is not a lot of information about this,
and there are many conflicting numbers,
but one figure that is used
is 209 fragging incidents
in 1970.
This is a low-ball number by some estimates,
Fragmentary information, one might say.
That's just in one year.
Fragging was the term

used when enlisted men
took action against their own officers,
or NCOs in a few cases,
sometimes killing them,
sometimes wounding them,
sometimes just expressing their views to them.
It's not surprising
that the government wouldn't want people to know
that it was not just North Vietnamese and Viet Cong
who were seen as the enemy.
Even if different sources disagree
on the true number—
and who knows how many went unreported?—
their very existence says a lot,
about the soldier's view of the war,
or about those leading it.

Day 210: Yo, can that thing fly?

The YO-3A
was a single-engine propeller plane
that had a 210 horsepower engine.
The 210 hp engine was muffled,
so the plane could fly
almost without being heard from the ground.
This made it a good scout plane.
It was an odd-looking thing,
developed for this war,
but it was so effective
it was used in law enforcement
back home
later on.
So it really was
good enough for government work.

Day 211: Once upon a time…

The final version
of the tales collected
by the Brothers Grimm,
Jacob and Wilhelm,
totaled 211,
although at least 32 more
would come out eventually.
The young men fighting this war
heard many of these tales
when they were growing up.
About frog kings
and adventurous children
and evil step-mothers
and princes and princesses
and witches
and fair maidens.
These weren't the only fairy tales
these guys heard,
and they weren't the only ones
they believed.

Day 212: Boiling over

212 degrees
(Fahrenheit, not kilometers)
is the boiling point of water.
And
it was about 212 days
that the North Vietnamese
planned the Tet offensive,
from sometime in '67 to
February of '68.
Give or take a day or two.
Yeah, a lot of things boiled over then.

Day 213: More casualties

213 is the total
of the ages of the five Americans
who immolated themselves to protest the war.
This honor roll includes:
Alice Herz, 82,
Norman Morrison, 31, who handed his daughter to someone just
before setting himself on fire outside Robert McNamara's window
at the Pentagon,
Roger Allen LaPorte, 22,
Florence Beaumont, 55,
George Winne Jr., 23.
That does not even include
people from other countries
who weren't too happy
about the war.

Day 214: DD214

You might not know it now, GI,
but when you do return to civilian life,
there will be a form DD214 for you,
that thing you signed to get the hell out.
It tells anyone who looks at it
that you were in the service
and what you did while you were in the service.
So it will be
an important document
for you to keep.
But
it also tells things
you didn't realize it told,
but see days 217, 251, and 258 for an idea of that.

Day 215: And in this corner...

... at 215 pounds,
The heavyweight champion of the world:
Muhammad Ali/Joe Frazier.
Muhammad Ali,
once and future Champ,
weighing in at 215 pounds
for the Fight of the Century
against Joe Frazier,
here and now Champ,
weighing in at 205,
in Madison Square Garden, on March 8th, 1971.

What do you mean
when you say two-fifteen?
That was not the latest
Weight for The Greatest.
And when they say Joe was smokin'
they ain't just ajokin'.
It must be repeated
they were both undefeated.
They both stood up tall,
refusin' to fall.

And Ali bounds out of his corner quickly ...
... one-time heavyweight Champ ...
... but stripped of his title ...
... for not stepping forward at the draft board ...
... but stepping forward against Frazier ...
... and still moving to his left ...
... still the showman ...
... but deadly serious about winning this bout ...
And out of his corner comes Frazier ...
... officially recognized as Champ ...
... looking to hold his title ...

... and prove his worth ...
... he looks angry ...
... he looks determined ...
... just as serious as his opponent ...

Ladies and gentlemen,
the winner,
and undisputed Heavyweight Champion of the World,
by unanimous decision,
Joe Frazier.
But
The saga does not end there.

On October 1st, 1975,
in the Philippines,
The Greatest,
now the defending Champ,
looking to hold his title,
comes out of his corner
weighing 224 pounds
and as pretty as ever
for the Thrilla in Manila.
And Smokin' Joe,
looking to regain his title,
comes out of his corner
still smokin'
at 215 pounds.

There's Frazier ...
... moving and punching ...
... there's Ali ...
... moving and punching ...
... and there's heat ...
... not moving, but punching ...
... doing as much damage ...
... as both of these ...

… brave fighters …
…do to each other …
… and it's hot …
… and it's hotter …
… and it's hotter still …

Ladies and gentlemen,
the winner
and undisputed Heavyweight Champion of the World
by Technical Knockout
before the 15th round,
Muhammad Ali.

And after the fight was over,
weighing 215 pounds,
Muhammad Ali.
And weighing closer to 200 pounds,
Joe Frazier.

Floatin' and Smokin',
Smokin' and Floatin'.
It wasn't about
Any showboatin'.
The struggle was historical,
Literal and metaphorical.

So, the epic of the two great fighters ended
Around the same time
As the story of the war they had somehow come to symbolize:
Ali of the left-wing, anti-establishment, anti-war, pro-civil rights
    folk,
Saying he had no beef with the Viet Cong,
His refusal of induction,
His prolonged, but eventually successful,
Battle through the courts
While he lost those prime years of his career;

Frazier somehow having become the great hope
Of the pro-war, conservative faction,
Even though, as a black man,
He was hardly opposed to the cause of civil rights.
He just wanted to fight the best, and be the best.
And believe it or not,
Smokin' Joe supported
The Greatest's refusal to serve.

In between, they fought a non-title bout
that had more clinching than punching
(and for the record, The Greatest won, making him Champ, 2-1).
So let's forget that one
and remember the good stuff:
The Immortals,
Opponents but not enemies,
Toe to toe
Doing honor to themselves and each other.
The Fight of the Century.
The Thrilla in Manila.

Day 216: Counting the bodies

The total of American KIA
(by the way, that's "Killed In Action")
in 1964
was 216.
That was the last year
it would be below four figures
until 1972.

Day 217: Tumult and oppression

Verse 217
of the Surat
Al-Baqarah

of the Holy Qur'an
concerns fighting in prohibited time,
which is a grave offense,
although it is graver to prevent access to the path of Allah.
And if any turn back from the faith
and die in unbelief,
their works will bear no fruit.

Day 218: Back in D.C.

Record Group 218
was the collection of records
of the U.S. Joint Chiefs of Staff.
Hot sounds from the Joint Chiefs?
No, not that kind of record.
The paper kind.

Day 219: Halfway along the azimuth

Lyndon: I sure would like for us to sit down and talk.
Alexei: I would like that too.
Lyndon: So why don't we do that?
Alexei: All right. Where?
Lyndon: Well, I can't really come to Moscow any time soon.
Alexei: Well I can't just come running to Washington now.
Lyndon: But you're in New York for a few days. I'd hate to let that
    opportunity slip by.
Alexei: Yes, I'm speaking at the UN in an effort to have Israel
    branded the aggressor in the Six Day War. But why don't you
    come up to New York while I'm here?
Lyndon: I'm not sure I want to do that. There would be way too
    much noise from people protesting the Vietnam conflict for us
    to talk.
Alexei: Yes, I'd been meaning to speak to you about that.

Lyndon: Well, there's that, but we have so much more to talk about. So how about it?

Alexei: I can't just go to you, right there in your yard.

Lyndon: Well, I hate to let this goldang opportunity pass us by. There must be some way to meet halfway.

Alexei: Halfway sounds good to me.

Richard: How about I give you a meeting place?

Alexei: Who he?

Lyndon: Alexei, let me introduce Richard Hughes, governor of the fine state of New Jersey.

Alexei: Ah yes, the state you can see from the Statue of Liberty. So, how is that halfway?

Lyndon: Dick, can you help us out here?

Richard: How about this. Alexei—you don't mind if I call you Alexei for the purposes of this exchange?...

Alexei: That's fine, Dick. After all, we're meeting halfway.

Richard: ... Alexei is staying at the Soviet representative's residence for his UN visit. And such a place is considered to be the visiting country's home soil. So, Premier Kosygin is on Soviet territory. And President Johnson is in the American capital.

Alexei: Daaa... (Yeeess...)

Lyndon: Okay, get on with it.

Richard: So, we in the Garden State can offer a place that is about halfway between New York, or the Soviet Union's territory there, and the White House. We happen to have an institution of higher learning there, with many fine buildings, Glassboro State College. I'm thinking specifically of Hollybush Mansion, a historic building that offers good meeting rooms in a dignified setting.

Lyndon: Well, I surely can make it to Glassburg.

Richard: Glassboro.

Lyndon: Whatever. Alexei?

Alexei: Sounds good to me. So, what is the compass heading from the USSR/New York to this Glassboro? And is that anything like the Politburo?

Richard: It's compass heading 219. But you don't need that. You can just follow the New Jersey Turnpike. And no it isn't.

Lyndon: Gosh darn it! I'm liking this better all the time.

Alexei: All right, but my aides tell me this New Jersey Turnpike gets very congested with traffic.

Lyndon: Not to worry, Alexei. You and your escort will be the only cars on the road at the time. You won't hit any traffic at all. Isn't that right, Dick?

Richard: That's right, Lyndon. We'll close off the entire road. And Alexei, you won't even have to stop at the toll booth.

Alexei: Toll booth. Some kind of capitalist bourgeois device, I assume?

Lyndon: Ne vazhno, Alexei. Never you mind. We have people to work out those kinds of details. So, how about it? Do we have a date?

Alexei: We do indeed, Lyndon. June 23 to 25, 1967. And I'm impressed with your Russian.

Lyndon: Aw, shucks. Warn't nothing. I'm looking forward to this. I foresee it being called the "Spirit of Glassboro" and helping to ease relations between our countries.

Alexei: Yes. I can see it now: "Glassboro-nost." I'm anticipating three days of talks, the first of which will be just the two of us and our interpreters, and a total of ten hours altogether. And I know we will be able to say afterward that our talks were *plodotvory*.

Lyndon: Will be what?

Interpreter: Fruitful, Mr. President.

Lyndon: Dang right they will.

Alexei: Although you understand your bombing of North Vietnam will still be a *kamen' pretknoveniya*.

Lyndon: Let me guess. That means what we call a sticking point.

Alexei: That's right.

Lyndon: I get that, but we'll make the best of what we have. I'm feeling better already. Dick, I want to thank you for this. I'll have to have you out to the LBJ Ranch some time. Or if not that, we'll have to settle for the White House.

Richard: You're quite welcome, Lyndon. And Alexei, I'm
    looking forward to meeting you then. I'm sure you'll like
    Glassboro.
Alexei: I am sure also, Dick. This will go down in history.

And it did.

Day 220: Fast strike

On the ground
hear the sound
of the Cobra,
Shelby Cobra.
Tearing up the highways of the Western world.
Over there,
in the air,
is a Cobra,
Huey Cobra.
A specialized attack helicopter for the eastern world.
Kind of small,
all in all,
is this Cobra,
Huey Cobra.
With the engine, rotor and transmission of a transport helicopter.
It got there
through the air,
this here Cobra,
Huey Cobra.
Acting as an escort for troop- or cargo-carrying choppers.
So streamlined
they would find
the new Cobra,
Huey Cobra,
that it could reach speeds of 220 miles per hour.

Along about 1967,

they came up with
a specialized attack helicopter for Vietnam.
It was a the AH-1 Huey Cobra,
better known just as the Cobra.
It looked kind of small for a chopper,
but it could move.
It had a maximum speed of about 220 miles an hour.
It used the engine, rotor, and transmission
of a transport helicopter,
with a new streamlined fuselage.
It acted as an escort
for troop- or cargo-carrying choppers.

221: Demonstrably upset

In 1968,
(yet again)
the National Student Association
(or NSA, but a different NSA from the NSA)
reported that 221 major demonstrations took place
at 101 colleges
involving 39,000 students,
which would be 2.6 percent
of American college enrollment.
This report came
the year after it was revealed
that the CIA (yeah, that CIA)
had been giving financial support
(and apparently quite a lot of it)
to the NSA (yes, the National Student Association)
since 1950.
After the outcry,
the CIA agreed to end its financing,
and the NSA (the National Student Association, that is)
said it would pay rent for its Washington, D.C., office.

Day 222: Biology lesson

For all that foliage
that you walked through,
flew over,
chopped down,
burned,
rearranged,
or just cursed,
now you can know,
that Vietnam has 222 species of fauna.
Doesn't that make it all seem worthwhile?

Day 223: Not wall-to-wall wall

Modern research indicates
that the Great Wall of China
actually has 223 miles of trenches
out of its 5,500 or so total miles.
Either way,
it's a lot of miles.
Seems to have done a pretty good job.

Day 224: While you're complaining about the heat...

If this is any consolation,
in 1963,
the coldest winter in 224 years
struck Britain,
known as the Big Freeze of 1963.
It was worse in England and Wales
than it was in Scotland.
It even went as low

as minus-19.4 Celsius
(that's minus-2.9 Fahrenheit,
for those of you who can't convert pounds sterling).

Day 225: Meanwhile

There were other things going on the world.
Englishman Francis Chichester
was out to sea for 225 days
before he returned home
the next day
from sailing around the world single-handed,
on the Gipsy Moth IV, a 53-foot ketch,
in 1967.
He would be knighted by Queen Elizabeth
for being the first person
to sail the world solo by the clipper route
(sailing around Africa and heading east).
There's no indication that he stopped in Vietnam.

Day 226: American losses

226 Native Americans died
serving in Vietnam.
They're forgotten about sometimes,
maybe because we are conditioned to think of them
as fighting against the U.S. Army,
and not on the same side.
So in this war
if the cavalry comes to the rescue
there could be Indians in the cavalry
riding to the rescue.
Cue the music.

Day 227: Mike forces

MACV authorized
what were called Mobile Strike Force Commands
or MSFC
or Mike forces,
in each of the four Corps tactical zones
and a fifth at Nha Trang
in 1965.
They had
an elite
airborne-qualified
227-man headquarters/service company
staffed by either Nungs or ethnic Cambodians,
both being prized soldiers.
There was also a permanent A-team,
several 552-man CIDG battalions
and a 135-man recon company.

Day 228: "Good evening, Mr. and Mrs. America, and all the ships at sea"

The National Association of Broadcasting
estimated that there were
228 programs in broadcasting
in American colleges
in 1975.
This would involve
17,250 students.
In 1960,
it had been 2,600 students
in 98 programs.
See what a difference
a Living Room War makes?
17,250 young people

eager
to go on the air
and tell the American people what a lousy idea the war was
after the people had already decided that for themselves.
And all those years Morley Safer spent
as a voice crying in the wilderness.

Day 229: The best years of somebody's life

The Veterans Administration
published a book of its own history,
Fifty Fabulous Years.
The book included the fact
that there were 229 veterans
who had made claims that were under study
for exposure to radiation after witnessing tests
from the end of World War II to 1963.

Day 230: Another precinct heard from

It was by 230 votes
that Senator Eugene McCarthy
lost the 1968 New Hampshire primary
to President Lyndon Johnson.
Understand,
McCarthy lost,
and yet that result is considered decisive
in Johnson's announcement
that he should/would not seek/accept
his party's nomination
as our president.
And what's even crazier
is that many analysts think
that a lot of those people who voted for McCarthy
were not supporting his anti-war campaign.

They were just kind of unhappy
and wanted to show it somehow.

Day 231: Thieu much (was not enough?)

231 was the flight number
of the C118 airplane
that evacuated former president
Nguyen Van Thieu
and his gold
out of South Vietnam
on April 25, 1975,
just before the North Vietnamese took over.
He didn't think it wise to stick around.
But he did see fit to criticize the USA
for failing to support him,
saying our withdrawal was
"an inhumane act by an inhumane ally."
That sounds like
a lack of gratitude.
Or, as Roger Grimsby said on New York's Channel 7
    Eyewitness News,
stopping just short of cursing the crosses on the graves of the
    Americans who died there.
Yeah, that's the guy we wanted running things.
Apparently $200 billion and more than 58,000 American lives,
not to mention a rigged election,
didn't add up to quite enough to keep him happy.
Guess that's why he relocated to England.
I mean, can you blame him,
after the way we treated him?

Day 232: Rough week

U.S. casualties
announced for

the week ending March 10, 1967
were 232 killed in action, and 1,381 wounded.
It was the highest for any week
of the war.
Up to that time.

Day 233: Talking about real money

An intelligence memo
by the Directorate of Intelligence, CIA,
in May of 1967
said that the total damage
inflicted on North Vietnam by U.S. bombing
was $233 million.
Oh, the same memo said
that the North Vietnamese had a high capability
to recover from the damage
by a combination of increased imports, dispersal, and fast repair.
While we're on 233,
that's the estimate in billions (with a b this time)
of the cost to the U.S. government
for veterans' benefits,
and that is not counting
the stuff we talked about on Day 14.
And,
While we're at it,
page 233 of the "Pacification Program" handbook
(see Day 86)
outlines the "basic liberties"
we were there to protect
as part of our WHAM.

Day 234: Canine contribution

Sometimes dogs were used
in a variety of ways.

they could be scouts
or trackers.
We think of them all being German Shepherds,
but there were other breeds too,
including Labs.
Believe it or not,
234 of them were killed in combat.
And don't forget to check Day 296.

Day 235: Nuclear familiarity

Just so you know,
the fissile isotope of uranium used in the first atom bomb
was U-235.

Day 236: Getting them young

The Air Force lost
236 first lieutenants.
More young people die,
and you might say
these young people hardly got their lives started,
barely got off the ground,
as it were.

Day 237: From Te Deum to Dies Irae

237 Catholic bishops
were in Rome for an Ecumenical Council
when JFK was in Dallas
on that dreadful day.

Day 238: Senate intelligence

In late 1975,
a Senate Intelligence Committee report
found that the FBI
conducted 238 burglaries
against "domestic subversive targets"
over a 26-year period
and then
tried to hide or destroy evidence
of these "clearly illegal" activities.
Those folks who broke into
an FBI office
knew that in 1971,
but it took the senators until 1975
to figure it out.
The intelligence of our elected leaders.

Day 239: Protecting the wildlife

In March of 1973,
representatives of 80 nations
signed a treaty restricting trade
of 239 animals,
as well as 375 endangered wildlife animal species.

Day 240: Fond in the hearts of so many

The Oakland Army Base,
which was the final U.S. stop for so many,
would close in 1999.
But a few years later,
the California Department of Transportation
would set aside $240 million

for redevelopment of the base.
Imagine the possibilities.

And on this day
begins planning for the flight
that will bring it all home,
125 days from now.

Day 241: Lots of heft

241 pounds was the maximum weight
for any male to enter the service
if he was 17 to 20 years old
and 78 inches tall
(that's 6 feet, 6 inches, if what you do to one side of the
    equation you must do to the other).
That's one pound more
than Arnold Schwarzenegger weighed
when he won
the IFBB Mr. Universe competition in 1969.

Day 242: Be it resolved

So while there's fighting going on here,
back at the UN,
somebody's passing Resolution 242.
Not that it means anything to anyone here.
That 242 is meant to get the Arabs and Israelis to stop fighting.
So they're trying to stop the fighting
in a hot, dry, dusty place,
while we would like to see an end to the fighting
stuck in a hot, wet, sweaty place,
except in the dry season when it's hot and dry and dusty,
and always humid.

And the talking continues in temperate New York.
New York, temperate?
You want to try that one again?

Day 243: Operation Babylift

One operation
that wasn't a military engagement
was Operation Babylift,
an attempt
to evacuate children
from South Vietnam
as the North Vietnamese closed in,
in 1975.
They were being brought
to the USA,
as well as other countries,
that were not Vietnam.
One flight,
out of Tan Son Nhut
on April 4,
was carrying 243 passengers.
It crashed just after takeoff,
killing more than 100 people,
most of them children
being rescued.

Day 244: Read alla 'bout it, Part 2

Occasionally,
newspapers would find their way
to the grunts
as well as to the rear echelon.

The brass
generally didn't mind
GIs reading those papers,
because they gave all the good news
about the war
and about the military.
However,
there were other newspapers
the brass didn't know about,
or approve if they did know about them.
244 by some counts,
although that is a rough estimation
because not all of them were known about
and some didn't last long.
They took an "alternative" view
of the war
and of military life.
A less than unfavorable view
of the use of drugs,
or of laxity in the ranks,
for example.
Some even provided information
about safe havens
for deserters.
Oh yes.

Day 245: A little light reading

The Watergate hearings
got a real jolt
in June of 1973,
when John Dean gave
a 245-page statement.
It took everything
to a whole new level.

Now a soldier's spirit is keenest in the morning; by noonday it has begun to flag; and in the evening, his mind is bent only on returning to camp.

Sun Tzu, *The Art of War*

Days 246 and 247: Genuine wall to wall

Two days.
So we're going to have two walls,
really two sections of one wall.
Each one
is 246.75 feet in length.
Meeting at an angle of 125 degrees, 12 minutes.
148 panels.
A lot of people objected
to Maya Lin's creation.
What did they want,
a statue of Winged Victory?
What better way to commemorate
a war that took so much
and gave so little?
Except heartache;
it gave plenty of that.
The statues were fine,
but the Wall has the names.
And this time,
the prose is the poetry.

Day 248: Where all roads lead

Trying to keep track
of every different coup
can make you coup-coup.
Look at Rome, for example.
It was in 248 A.D.
that the Roman Empire celebrated
one thousand years since its founding.
The Romans said that Romulus
started things off on April 21, 753 B.C.
If you say so.

The emperor for this millennial celebration
was Philip the Arab,
or Marcus Julius Philippus Augustus
to those of you using the old calendar.
Philip the Arab,
who became emperor
when Gordian got knotted up,
didn't get too far into the next millennium.
He was overthrown by Decius
in September of 249.
Sic transit grandeur.

Day 249: Leaving the country for health reasons

In Japan,
far from this war
but close to it,
was the 249th General Hospital
at Camp Drake
in Asaka,
outside Tokyo.
Originally it had been
an Imperial Japanese Army training facility.
After we took it over,
it was named after an officer
who was killed liberating the Philippines.
During this war,
it treated about 1,000 patients a month.

Day 250: Special services

It wasn't all guns
and bombs,

or even medicine
and money.
U.S. Special Services
set up 250 field library units,
arranging the distribution
of 190,000 magazine subscriptions
and 350,000 paperbacks.
So at least there was something to read.

Day 251: Putting a spin on the duty to one's country

What they didn't tell you,
when they finally handed you your DD214,
was that there was this number on it.
Right there in that line
about Reason and Authority
for Transfer or Discharge Data,
was this SPN,
meaning Separation Program Number.
And this number, commonly referred to as a Spin,
told anyone who had a list of the numbers
—and many people, including employment interviewers, did—
things about you, things you might not have been aware
that anyone knew about you.
It was sort of a secret,
to discharged veterans, anyway.
So, one Spin number
was 251.
Punitive discharge. Class I homosexual-general court martial.
For those of you keeping track,
homosexuality is also mentioned
in SPNs 252, 253, 255, 256, and 257.
Guess that one was really on someone's mind.
But there will be more days
after this one.

Day 252: Dak Son

The Degar people,
The ones we called Montagnards,
pretty much wanted
to be left to themselves.
That didn't work
for a lot of people,
on both sides of the DMZ,
so the Montagnards did what they thought
worked best for them.
It didn't always help.
In 1967 the North Vietnamese
killed 252 Montagnards in the village of Dak Son
an event known as the Dak Son Massacre,
for cooperating with the South.
Supposedly, the largest community of Montagnards
outside southeast Asia,
is in Greensboro, N.C.

Day 253: Break time

Nothing today.
Smoke 'em if you got 'em.

Day 254: Certain standards

Just in case you need to know this,
a tennis ball is tested for bounce
by being dropped
254 centimeters
(that's 100 inches in dog years)
onto concrete.
Not 253 centimeters,

but 254.
A bounce between 135 and 147 centimeters
(that's 53 to 58 inches, for those of you keeping score at home)
is considered acceptable.

Day 255: Training session

All right, listen up again.
The number 255 is a mersenne number,
and the smallest perfect totient number
that is neither a power of three nor thrice a prime.
It is also the largest number
that can be represented
in an 8-bit unsigned integer.
Any questions?

Day 256: More death at home

256 people were killed
on an oil drilling rig near Boothville, La.,
by Hurricane Camille,
in April of 1969.
Camille really got around.
At least 189 people died
in floods and landslides in Virginia.

Day 257: Family photos

In 1955,
The year direct U.S. assistance in south Vietnam began,
master photographer Edward Steichen
examined the work of 257 documentary photographers,
from 68 countries,

in organizing
The Family of Man,
a Museum of Modern Art chronicle
of life from birth to death.
It would be seen by 9 million people.
Pretty big family.

Day 258: This one will make your head spin

Here's a great SPN.
258:
Ineptitude.
Ineptitude? For what,
Killing?
This seems like an SPN
they could have worn out in no time.
Who do I have to see
to get this one?
I mean, it can't be that hard
to be inept.
It could also mean:
Unfitness, multiple reasons.
Yeah, I bet there were a lot of those.

Day 259: For Conspicuous Gallantry

Of all the people sent over there,
259 won the highest award possible,
the Congressional Medal of Honor.
For "conspicuous gallantry and intrepidity
at the risk of his life above and beyond
the call of duty ..."
They did it in a variety of ways.
One of them was an admiral.

You wonder,
Did they stop and think on it,
or did they just do it?
Real achievement,
in a place where they handed out medals
like wooden nickels.
But not all of those 259
received the medals themselves.
Their families did.
Like the family of Milton Olive,
the first African-American of the war to receive it,
who sacrificed himself
and got a field at Fort Polk named after him.

You wonder.

Of course,
This number
Is arrived at kind of late.
How late?
September of 2014.
That's pretty late.
Yeah, but it includes
eight honorees
among the Valor 24.
Twenty-four guys,
eight Vietnam veterans,
who did something to deserve the Medal of Honor
but who,
somehow or other,
didn't receive it, until March of 2014.
Maybe they just weren't American enough.
Too Black
or too Hispanic
or too Jewish.
But since then, there were three more.

And who knows, maybe there will be more yet.
But at least maybe we're seeing
the light at the end of the tunnel.

You wonder.

Day 260: Snakes, in the grass, and wherever else

We've already learned
about the fauna growing here.
Now,
you think you saw a lot
of snakes, lizards, and whatever else
while you were walking around?
It turns out Vietnam has
260 reptile species.
Yup,
all those pit vipers,
and cobras,
and whatever else
you ran across
were just a few
of those 260.
I didn't think there were 260 reptile species
in the whole world.
And this is just one small part of the world,
even if it isn't
The World.

Day 261: Not bad for an interim leader

Pope John XXIII
(now Saint, by causing a second miracle)

was the 261st pope (officially).
He was intended by many
to be an interim pope.
Instead, he called the Second Vatican Council,
which substituted for the second miracle,
and had quite an effect, beyond his lifetime.
He is even honored in the Anglican Communion.
He also wrote "Pacem in Terris"
or "Peace on Earth" for those of you requiring
	simultaneous translation.
He also intervened for peace
during the Cuban Missile Crisis,
those scary thirteen days
when everyone wondered
and worried.
He poured holy oil
on troubled American waters.
"Pacem In Terris" was
different, in that,
unlike most papal encyclicals,
it was addressed not just to Catholics
but to "all men of good will."
In that, he said something
that was picked up by the guys
from Day 59:
That human life is "infinitely precious."
And this pope
and the American president,
a Catholic no less,
shared the same first name
and died the same year.
How 'bout that?

Day 262: No rush, catch as catch can

262 pass receptions.
Not bad, I guess.
So who had that?
Well, it was
Jim Brown.
Jim Brown?
Of the Cleveland Browns?
The one who retired holding
the NFL single-season
and career
rushing records,
as well as the record
for rushing touchdowns?
The guy who defined running?
That Jim Brown?
The very same.
And he was the same one
who didn't run
but walked away,
trading his place on the gridiron
for one on the movie set,
exchanging the sweaty eleven
for the Dirty Dozen
at his own pace
and under his own terms.
To the shock,
consternation,
and bafflement
of many,
and the delight of others.
He had a lot of ways to make it happen.

Day 263: NSAM

We got this thing called
a National Security Action Memo.
NSAM.
Well, NSAM 263,
issued on October 11, 1963,
was a formal directive
for a policy of withdrawal of U.S. troops from Vietnam
and for the mission to be completed
no later than 1965.
This was kept kind of quiet,
as was JFK's directive
that no announcement be made
of plans
to withdraw
one thousand
military personnel by the end of the year.
At the time NSAM 263 was written,
American KIAs in Vietnam
were around 200,
give or take.
But there were other days after this one,
weren't there?
Like Day 273, for example.

Day 264: Close that door, there's a draft, eastern seaboard

On December 5, 1967,
264 people,
Out of 1,000 in attendance,
were arrested
while attempting to close down
the armed forces induction center in New York City.

Those arrested included
Dr. Benjamin Spock, he of baby care fame, and poet
    Allen Ginsburg.
Spock would be indicted a month later,
along with the Rev. William Sloan Coffin,
for conspiracy to aid and abet draft evasion.
(You can get arrested for that?)
But then we have to cross the country,
to get to Day 268.

Day 265: Wearing the belt

The official weight
of Bruno Sammartino,
who was
the longest-reigning
heavyweight wrestling champion of the world,
was 265 pounds.
Of course, that was during a time
when these "exhibitions"
were less glitzy
and more gritty
than nowadays.
That was when the card included
Killer Kowalski
and Gorilla Monsoon (not to be confused with a
    Vietnamese monsoon)
and Nature Boy Buddy Rogers
and Golden Boy Arnold Skaalen
and Vern Gagne
and Red, not to mention Lou, Bastien (or bastion)
and Sailor (or Seaman) Art Thomas
and Haystacks Calhoun going against tag teams,
and when Skull Murphy lived in a trailer park
on Route 1 in Edison, New Jersey.

The days when the women wrestlers,
like Princess Moola,
were notable more for their brawn
than for how they looked in skin-tight,
not to mention minimal,
outfits.
Or the midgets,
like Sky-Low Lowe.
Well, something's lost, but something's gained.
Oh, for the days
when you could cheer the good guys
and boo the bad guys
because they were so easy to tell apart.

Day 266: We're down to double figures!

On this day let us stop for reflection,
Dressed right, covered down for inspection.
The statistics don't lie.
They say warriors die.
I'm only twenty, I'll be the exception.

A telegram from Secretary of State Dean Rusk
to U.S. Ambassador to Vietnam Henry Cabot Lodge,
on December 6, 1963,
said the number of VC incidents
in the first half of 1963
was 266 per week
It was 363 in 1962.

Well that's nice,
but do I really care?
I'm down under 100.
I'm short.
Just shy of a century of days,

days that will feel like centuries,
but it's getting closer.
Ninety-nine bottles of beer on the wall.

Day 267: All aboard?
(Binh there, Dinh that.)

It's 267 miles
(or 430 kilometers, if you're using base 12)
from Ho Chi Minh City
(which we so fondly recall as Saigon,
converting from metric)
to the province of Binh Dinh.
Binh Dinh.
In the South Central Coast region.
Might have been the landing place
of the first people to come to
what is now Vietnam.
Coastal,
but with lush green mountains and forests.
Even described as a paradise.
In 1966,
we needed to relocate people living there
into "refugee"
aka "concentration"
camps,
so they wouldn't become communist.
Lot of them didn't want to go.
So we had to persuade them.
To do that, *mon ami*,
we bombed the shit out of them,
but we got them to move, pretty much.
Shelling also destroyed coconut trees,
which might have put a dent in our piña coladas,
but it definitely put a hurt on their economy,

depending as it did on coconuts.
WHAM (yet again),
Bam
Nam (sight rhyme).
Place wasn't quite such a paradise
for a while
after that.
But it's only 267 miles
(or 430 clicks, in piasters)
by rail
to Ho Chi Minh City.

Day 268: Shutting out the draft, on the left coast

268 protesters
were arrested while trying
to block
the induction center
in Oakland, California,
on December 18th and 19th, 1967.
This was out of 750 people who were there.
Imagine what they would have thought
if they could see a month and a half ahead.

Day 269: A different kind of vine

In 1968,
you remember that year,
the world production of wine
reached 269.3 million hectoliters.
Hectoliters?
100 liters.
That's a hecto lot of liters.

So that's how many glasses?
Let's see, if a glass holds ...
Oh the hell with it. You do the math.
I'm an enlisted man.
Why not just drink it from the bottle?
Because
no matter how you count it,
it isn't likely
that many of those hectoliters
will make their way to the boonies.

Day 270: End of a trimester

It's 270 days.
A child conceived on Day One,
a product of love,
or parting,
or opportunity,
or even cash exchange,
would be born today,
or so they say.
Two-hundred, eighty days
of becoming.
Give or take a day or two.
Give or take a life or two.
The kids fighting here
were born 270 days after the war
(give or take a day, a month, or a year or two),
the big one, WW 2.
So the babies who were born after the Great Crusade was over
got to fight in the not-so-great crusade.
Which war will today's baby have to fight?

You wonder.

Day 271: Hitting the heartland

The Midwest,
Middle America,
the nation's heartland,
was hit in many ways,
including the number of boys who went off to war
and didn't come back.
It was also hit in 1965
with a series of tornadoes
that killed 271 people.

Day 272: Of the people, by the people, for the people

The battle of Gettysburg was fought,
between North and South,
from July first through third
in 1863.
Four months later,
President Abraham Lincoln
delivered what is now known as
The Gettysburg Address.
272 words.
It took him about two minutes.
The battle was considered one of the most important in the
    Civil War,
And it lasted three days,
and Honest Abe's speech
still stands as a model of clarity
and sincerity.
272 words.

Day 273: NSAM 273

NSAM 273
was drafted within 24 hours
of JFK's death.
It emphasized
the continuity of policy
between JFK and LBJ.
So they were going to keep going
the way Kennedy had.
Or were they?
We'll never know for sure.
One more frustration.

Day 274: Don't go spending that money

SPN 274 is:
Physical disability resulting
from intentional misconduct or
willful neglect or
incurred during period of unauthorized absence.
Not entitled to severance pay.

Day 275: Old campaigners

Campaign 275
was a North Vietnamese
attempt to seize the Central Highlands
during the Final Offensive of 1975.
A big part of Campaign 275
was the assault on Ban Me Thuot,
the capital city of Darlac Province
and the largest urban concentration
in the Central Highlands.

There was intense fighting,
but by March 12, 1975,
the North Vietnamese controlled the city,
leaving no ARVN troops between Ban Me Thuot and the
      South China Sea.
And the rest is
the rest.

Day 276: Widening our horizons

276 people,
American, Cambodian, and others
had to be evacuated
from the U.S. embassy in Phnom Penh, Cambodia,
in April of 1975,
as Khmer Rouge forces approached.
Congress refused President Ford's request
for military aid for Lon Nol.
By this time,
there were no more U.S. troops in Indochina,
and Congress didn't want to risk
sending any back.
And besides,
the North Vietnamese were making steady gains at home.
The Cambodian civil war
would go on to kill one in eight people.
A month after Congress's refusal,
Ford signed a proclamation
terminating wartime veterans benefits,
saying the U.S. was no longer at war.

Day 277: Letting them do it themselves

Operation Lam Son 277
was one of about 29 such operations,

supposedly named after the birthplace
of Le Loi, a 15th-century Vietnamese nationalist.
They were supposed to be part of turning over the war
to the Vietnamese.
Anyway, this one,
in Quang Tri Province,
from April to June of 1969,
went all right,
with 541 enemy reported killed,
and no ARVN losses.
Of course, the most famous Lam Son was 719,
two years later,
but we already saw that
on Day 253.

Day 278: WHAM, Part 4

By 1973,
278 U.S. servicemen
were convicted in military courts
of serious offenses
against Vietnamese civilians.
Serious offenses?
How serious?
Murder,
negligent homicide,
and rape.
Oh, that serious.
Yeah.

Day 279: California contributin'

California,
the Golden State,
the third largest in area,

the 31st state admitted to the Union,
the state that wasn't most populous when the war started
but was by the time it ended,
the contiguous state closest to Vietnam,
gave the most in number of service members,
and most killed in action,
at a rate of 279
for every 10,000 of its population.

Day 280: More WHAM, Far East ally version

In the temple in Dien Nien,
In the schoolyard in Phuoc Binh,
In the Province of Quang Ngai
In the District of Son Tinh,
In the Year of the Horse.

By the South Korean forces
By their sheer determination,
By their weapons and projectiles
By the closest estimation:
By the time that it was over,
280 were dead.

Most were women, children, elders,
But there "might" have been VC there.
Best to not take any chances
And then leave without a fanfare.
October 9-10.

Day 281: Standing up for sitting down

On April 1 (no foolin') of 1964,
281 or so people were arrested

following civil rights demonstrations
in St. Augustine.
Included among the white people in the group,
which was trying to be seated
at a segregated restaurant,
was Mary Parkman Peabody,
the mother of the governor of Massachusetts.
Taking a stand, or seat,
at 72 years of age.
Wait a minute.
St. Augustine,
isn't that in Florida?
Yup.
Not in Mississippi or Alabama.
But in the oldest city
in this great land of ours.
Can you stand it?

Day 282: Junction City

Operation Junction City,
in February of 1967,
was one of the biggest of the war,
involving the 1st Infantry Division,
the 25th Infantry Division,
the 173rd Airborne (we had a day for them already)
and the 11th Armored Cavalry Regiment.
It was a no-kidding-around operation
that was going to find those commies
and make them fight
and give them a whuppin'
that they wouldn't soon forget,
and that would turn this war around.
Except they wouldn't co-operate.
They stayed away, declined the invitation, avoided us for the
    most part.

(Must have read *The Art of War*:
"If the enemy is superior in strength, evade him."
Or maybe they just didn't care for our company.
Was it something we said?)
and the losses they suffered weren't in
big pitched battles.
We found things like food and supplies,
but they kept right on going.
We had 282 killed.

Day 283: The bloodless war

In what would be something of a pattern,
Arnold Palmer and Jack Nicklaus
finished in a tie at 283
in the U.S. Open in 1962.
Palmer—The King—
and Nicklaus—the Golden Bear—
seemed to be doing that kind of thing
for much of the '60s and beyond.
If one didn't win, the other did.
They, and Gary Player, helped popularize golf,
making it more democratic, so to speak.
Funny thing is, that same year,
in the same state (Pennsylvania),
Player became the first non-resident of the U.S.
to win the PGA championship,
with a 278, beating Bob Goalby by one stroke.
As for the 1962 U.S. Open,
it went to an 18-hole playoff,
and Nicklaus won it,
71 to 74.

Day 284: Staple crop

In pre-French days,
In other words going way back,
individual holdings by rice-farmer families
in the Mekong Delta
yielded 284 metric tons of (polished) rice.
That grew to
1,454,000 metric tons.
Holdings ranged from two to twelve acres.
Cultivated rice land rose from 1,282 acres
to 5,450,000 acres from 1880 to 1939.

Day 285: Surface to air

285 pounds.
That was the warhead
packed in the SA-2 Guideline
surface-to-air missiles
the Soviets gave North Vietnam
to shoot down our planes.
And it threw its weight around pretty well.

Day 286: Spring Break

In 1970
(think of Kent State if it helps),
286 college campuses around the country
were shut down
by strikes or other actions
by the end of the spring semester.
448 campuses had been disrupted,
but the rest found a way to carry on.
It ain't quite Ft. Lauderdale,
but the police were still kept busy.

Day 287: Friendly fire

The number of Americans killed
in the battle of Dak To,
in 1967,
has been estimated as 287.
It ended when troops advanced
and learned the NVA 174th Regiment
had slipped out during the night.
As many as 42 of those KIA, many of them officers,
might have been killed when one of our bombs
landed
in the middle of our guys.

Day 288: Making the necessary corrections

In 1971,
the U.S. Mission in Saigon
announced it would devote $400,000
for the construction of
288 isolation cells
to replace the "tiger cages"
the South Vietnamese used
to confine prisoners at the Con Son Correction Center
on Con Son Island,
aka Poulo Condore.
The prisoners,
who were obstinate troublemakers confined temporarily,
were humanely treated.
At least that's what the South Vietnamese government said.
The Red Cross saw it differently.
It reported that the prisoners were not common criminals,
but POWs or Buddhist dissidents,
and they were abused while in prison.
A congressional delegation
found pretty much the same thing.

Day 289: Instructional

U.S. Department of State Instruction 289
(or Depins 289, if you, too, are into the brevity thing),
of June 6, 1949.
It would have been a memo to the French Foreign Office
saying that the U.S. determined
that the best chance for preserving the integrity of Indochina
was for France to give assurances
that Vietnam was to control its own destiny.
It sort of concluded that France couldn't do much else.
Depins 289 would have been a memo
if it was delivered,
but it wasn't,
because the U.S. ambassador to France
objected strongly,
saying it was too discouraging
and gave the impression
the U.S. would support France
only in the unlikely event of French success
in Vietnam.

Day 290: Fighting for peace, love, law, and order

Two hundred, ninety.
That's the number we have
for how many protesters
were arrested in Chicago
during the 1968 Democratic convention
(that year yet again).
That's about 100 more
than the number of police injured.
The irony there is
that the people who wanted to end the war

probably helped bring about the election
that would prolong it.
And the police who were there to uphold the law
were accused of being the worst lawbreakers.
Either way,
it was not the most edifying sight
for anyone to view.
Great television viewing, though.

Day 291: Haiku for a numberless day

In war, young men die.
Many more fight on again,
but they will die too.

Day 292: High-level communication

Two-niner-two.
They set up a camp.
RON.
Remain overnight.
NDP.
Night defensive perimeter.
Where you set up a defensive position,
Sort of a perimeter,
To remain, and rest?, overnight.
And they put up a two-niner-two.
That's that big antenna over there,
So we can keep in contact
With someone, back somewhere.
So we're never too far away.
And if you think it's big when it's all put together,
Wait until it's taken apart,
and put in a duffel bag

and someone has to carry it.
That is one heavy mother.
Maybe 292 means how much it weighs.
Shit, it's heavy.
Heavier than it is high.
And it's high.

Day 293: As if things weren't bad enough

Natural disasters
don't take time out
to pause for the affairs of humans.
293 people were killed
in flooding caused by
the worst monsoon rains in six years,
in the five northernmost provinces of South Vietnam,
October 30 and November 1, in 1970.
Not bombs,
or bullets,
or mines.
Fighting pretty much came to a standstill.
For a few days, anyway.

Day 294: What did you learn in school today?

A document from North Vietnam
listed a total of 294 schools in North Vietnam
that were bombed
or strafed
by American aircraft
from August of 1964
to September of 1966.
Hard lessons.
And the homework gets pretty rough too.

Day 295: The beat goes on. Another lament

In 1976,
we're out of the war,
and the killing has ceased,
for us, anyway.
In Northern Ireland though,
295 people were killed in the "Troubles"
that were just picking up momentum.
If it's
a foot for every year,
this will be one long coffin.
How is it that death and hatred
always find a way to keep going?
Will the world ever find
a day when the killing stops?
An dtiocfaidh an lá?

Day 296: Not just the dogs

In addition to those 234
brave dogs that died
in their country's service,
296 dog handlers
lost their lives as well.
Did it help or hurt them
to tend to a dog along with everything else?

Day 297: How ya gonna keep 'em?

In 1960,
the average size of an American farm was 297 acres.
A year later it was 306 acres.
By 1969 it was 390 acres,

and by 1975 it was 420 acres.
That doesn't mean there was more farmland,
just fewer of them, and bigger.
The U.S. farm population was 16 million in 1960.
Ten years later it was 10 million.

Day 298: More orchestrated

Not all the sounds coming from college campuses
were raucous.
In 1968 and 1969,
there were 298 college symphony orchestras
in the United States.
Their music was softer,
easier on the ear,
although that might be a matter of taste.

Day 299: Jolly good, no

In July of 1966,
by a vote of 299-230,
the British Parliament upheld
Prime Minister Harold Wilson's support
of American policy in Vietnam,
but disassociated Britain from U.S. bombing raids
on the Hanoi-Haiphong area.
Earlier, Parliament defeated, 331-230,
a move to commit Britain to supporting
U.S. policy on Vietnam without reservation.

Day 300: These boots were made
for the boonies

According to information released
by Goodyear Chemicals
jungle boots outlasted standard boots
by 300 percent.
Those are the ones with the canvas sides,
which dried out and didn't rot as quickly
as the plain old leather boots.
And they had that removable mesh thing in the sole.
Great traction and mileage too.
Not to mention the blimp.

Day 301: Keep on pumping

In 301 procedures in 1968-69,
heart surgeons used veins or arteries from a patient's own body
to reroute blood around clogged areas.
Coronary bypass became routine.
Not that it made much of a difference
in some parts of the world.

Day 302: A mighty fortress is
our watchtower

Number 302
of the Bach Werke Verzeichnis,
or Bach's work list,
(converting Deutschmarks to dollars)
is "Ein feste Burg ist unser Gott"
or "A Mighty Fortress is Our God"
(aubgesehen von den Linden)
adapted from Luther (he of Day 95),

adapted from Psalm 46.
Who knows,
maybe that music helped
someone deal with the day-to-day.
Not exactly the Brandenburg Concertos,
but then no one is confusing jungle foliage with Brandenburg.
But then again,
while we're also shpraching of Berlin,
302 is the number
of watchtowers along the Berlin Wall,
or die Berliner Mauer,
(to those of you who can't convert from the metric system)
more popularly known as the
Antifaschistischer Schutzwall,
or Anti-Fascist Protection Rampart,
(in layman's terms).
It kept all those happy East Germans
from getting fat by being force-fed western crullers,
or so they said
in the Kremlin
and Hohenschönhausen.
But we know that all along the watchtower
(maybe not this watchtower)
they was Dylan, Hendrix,
and a whole lot in between.

Day 303: Operational oversight

There was
the 303 Committee.
It was
a global covert operations oversight group,
and it was chaired by McGeorge Bundy.
The group got its name
because it met

in Room 303
of the Executive Office Building,
not because Kennedy had 303 electoral votes.
One can only imagine
what kind of discussions were held in that room,
not to mention what kind of decisions were made.

Day 304: Surprise, surprise, surprise

North Vietnam's 304th Division
got around a lot.
It had units at Hue
and at Khe Sanh,
where it was hit hard.
In April of 1972,
supported by Soviet tanks and artillery,
it took the northern half of Quangtri province,
causing an increase in the flow of refugees.
The whole thing caught American leaders
by surprise,
but the overall U.S. response
was a lack of concern.

Day 305: The longest journey starts…

305 American soldiers
were killed during what has come to be called
the Pleiku Campaign.
It was a month-long campaign
that included the engagement
in the Ia Drang valley.
That particular battle,
in 1965,
in addition to being immortalized in book and movie,

would prove to be significant,
even a foreshadowing
of what was to come.
For peace, as the poet says,
comes dropping slow.
Very slow.
Very, very slow.
Very, very, very
slow.

Day 306: Bombardment

The 306th Bombardment Wing
had strategic nuclear alert duties
with those B52s
under Operation Chrome Dome
(what, was it named after some bald guy?)
for the Strategic Air Command.
The unit was assigned conventional bombing operations
in southeast Asia
in 1966.
But it did both well enough
to win an Air Force Outstanding Unit award.
It came back home to Florida
in 1973
after the Paris Peace Accords
brought a halt to bombing.

Day 307: Operation Marigold

It was a Boeing 307 Stratoliner
that flew Janusz Lewandowski
on Operation Marigold.
Lewandowski was a Polish diplomat,

and that 307 was flying him between
Hanoi and Saigon,
and who knows where else,
exploring ways
to negotiate peace.
This was 1966.
It seems
the Soviets weren't really happy about the war either,
seeing it as a burden and a distraction.
The mission was unsuccessful,
possibly because of American mistakes,
including bombing railroads close to Hanoi.
But Lewandowski racked up the frequent flyer miles.

Day 308: War of maneuver

The Viet Minh
(they're the ones who fought the French)
had a 308th Division,
one of six put together
by General Giap
(remember him?)
in 1950.
It was a regular army,
based in the Tonkin area,
with the assignment to conduct a war of maneuver,
aimed at drawing French units into combat
in locales and under conditions
that favored the Vietnamese
by neutralizing French superiority
in firepower and air support.
It worked,
eventually.

Day 309: 309 cubes

In 1969,
American Motors,
which gave us the Rambler,
like what Lois Lane drove,
had a Rebel,
and an Ambassador,
with a 309 cubic inch engine.
Va-room!

Day 310: Biology lesson

So, we got the bamboo and other fauna.
And we know how many reptiles there are.
Now listen up yet again.
Vietnam is home
to 310 mammals.
That's 310 types of mammals.
You probably wouldn't see very many of them.
They're usually smart enough to run
when humans are coming.
Who would have even thought
there were that many animal species in existence?
But if you think that's good,
Think on this:
Vietnam has
almost as many nematode species.
Nematode species?
That means things like roundworms,
for those of you who were out having another cigarette during
science class.
See what you can learn in a year
when you pay attention.
Because who knows how many of those 310 or so species,

which tend to be a lot smaller than the mammals,
would wind up in your clothes
or your hair
or your food?
And you might not even know it,
for a while.

Day 311: Frequently flying

The Marines had
a jet Squadron 311.
It flew at least 50,000 combat sorties.
That is a whole lot
of combat sorties.

Day 312: Sharon Lane

It was the 312th Evacuation Hospital in Chu Lai
where Sharon Lane was working
when she was killed
on June 8, 1969.
Sharon Lane,
nurse,
first lieutenant, U.S. Army,
the only female service member
killed as a result of enemy fire,
a 122 mm rocket that hit
Ward 4 of the 312th Evac.
She had been in country two months.

Day 313: Good thing we weren't expanding the war

On October 29, 1972,
U.S. fighter bombers made
313 strikes against enemy positions in South Vietnam.
Meanwhile, North Vietnamese troops
were intensifying infiltration around Saigon.
This was at a time when we were pulling back,
decreasing our role in the war.
But at least,
we turned Long Binh Junction,
affectionately known as LBJ,
over to the South Vietnamese two weeks later.

Day 314: Eyes in the sky

Remember Sputnik?
Way back there in 1957,
them Russkies launched the
first artificial satellite, called Sputnik (which pretty much
     means Satellite).
And we were hot and bothered,
determined to catch up.
Well, by the end of 1968
(that year again)
the USSR had 314 identified satellites.
We had 544.
So I guess we caught up.

Day 315: Documentation

Document 315
was a telegram from

Secretary of State John Foster Dulles
in Geneva,
where the conference was taking place,
(which of course you remember from Day 17)
back to the State Department
in April of 1954.
It informed the folks back home
that England was refusing
to help stop communism in Vietnam,
meaning
England wasn't going to help France at Dien Bien Phu,
or anywhere else over there.
It seems
the Brits thought the French were destined to lose in Vietnam
and didn't want to go down with them.
This was one more thing
that didn't come from the Geneva Conference,
which the U.S. (meaning Dulles, who voted with his feet)
didn't like in the first place.

Day 316: Spearhead

The 316th Brigade
of the People's Army of Vietnam,
or the North Vietnamese,
was the spearhead unit
to move into Saigon to end the war.
The unit did its job.

Day 317: Play it again, and again

Bet you forgot all about this,
if you ever heard of it in the first place,
but Section 317 was part of

a public law
that outlawed payola,
which was a quaint term for
guys on the radio
taking extra money
under the turntable, as it were,
to give repeated air time
to certain songs,
the songs for which they were
payola-d.
There was a stink about it,
and so it became illegal.
Although who knows if that stopped it?
Same old song.

Day 318: Better than average

The guys we were helping,
the ARVN,
Army of the Republic of Vietnam,
had a Task Force 318.
It was part of the ARVN's
3rd Armored Cavalry Brigade.
And TF 318
was commanded
by Brigadier General Tran Quang Khoi,
who was considered,
by U.S. military leaders,
to be a good officer.
Unfortunately, the ARVN didn't have
quite enough of those.
The 3rd ACR took part
in the ARVN's last offensive
of the war,
trying to attack North Vietnamese forces
near Duc Hue.

Day 319: From one transition to another

319
is the approximate number
of days between
the assassination of Kennedy
and the removal of Khrushchev from power.
In a way,
both of them were instrumental
in what's going on during this war,
but neither of them was around
to watch it play out to the end,
although Nikita was around
eight years longer than Jack was.

Day 320: Marking on the curve

Another word from the economic experts.
320 economists
from 50 colleges
issued a statement
denouncing the Johnson administration's fiscal policies,
opposing any tax increase,
and asserting
that the war was a major source
of economic problems in the United States.

This was in January of 1968—
again. What is it about that year?
So anyway,
if there was a curve here,
were these guys ahead of it or behind it?

Day 321: Chopper down

Mama, what is that blocking the way?
Hush, child, just go and play.
Just playing is kind of hard
with that thing taking up all our yard.
I know it's not easy, but please understand
there are so many in our land.
So I will work and you will play.
We'll find a way, day by day.

To give you an idea
of how many helicopters
flew in the war,
think of this.
In 1966,
321 U.S. helicopters were lost.
That's just in 1966.

Day 322: CIP

The Commodity Import Program
or CIP,
was meant to boost the economy
in South Vietnam,
from 1955 to 1975,
by giving the government money
that would be made available to merchants.
The U.S. spent $322.4 million in economic aid
for South Vietnam,
in 1955.
About $280 million of that was through the CIP.
It might have been a great idea,
but it didn't work for improving the country,
although a few individuals did all right from it.

Day 323: Apple pie order

Norman Rockwell
drew 323 covers
for *The Saturday Evening Post.*
Some said he
captured the heart of America,
but others said he didn't.
Some said he was an artist,
but others (himself included)
said he was an illustrator.
Either way,
when he drew it,
people looked at it.
The *Post* ceased publication in 1969,
but Norman Rockwell kept drawing,
illustrating, whatever.
During World War II,
he drew pictures
of Rosie the Riveter,
who flexed her muscles at home,
and Willie Gillis,
who served in the Army.
Willie would have to stand
for all the American service members
in all the wars.

Day 324: Know your enemy

The People's Army of Vietnam
(the PAVN),
remember, that is the army of North Vietnam,
had a 324th Division,
in Nghe An Province.
It was tasked

with training infiltrators.
All in all you'd have to say,
looking back on every day,
over the hills and far away,
it did a pretty good job.

Day 325: Arma virumque cano…
or
Quo usque tandem abutere…

As usual,
Harvard,
JFK's alma mater,
was ahead of the curve.
In 1961,
police had to use tear gas
to break up a riot by students.
1961.
So they saw the mistake of the war even then?
Uh, no.
The students were protesting
Harvard's decision
to print its degrees in English
rather than in Latin.
This was changing a tradition
that went back 325 years.
Mucky-mucks said it would be hypocritical,
since Latin was no longer a required subject.
We decline to parse that one.
I mean, 325 years.
No Latin on the sheepskin.
And probably not a sheepskin either.
What's next,
admitting women?

Day 326: Standing tall

During much of this war,
the Boston Celtics dominated
the NBA.
But one season,
the 76ers,
from Philadelphia,
reached for it
and would not be denied.
The season started in 1966
and it ended in 1967
(so it's kind of like the 76ers in 67
or something like that).
Wilt Chamberlain.
The Stilt.
Who reached so high
and came so close,
so many times,
grabbed the prize this time.
It would be hard not to notice him anyway, but
he scored 326 points in 15 playoff games,
on 132 baskets
(no more than two points each)
out of 228 attempts.
And 437 rebounds
and 135 assists.
(He'd win another one in 1972
before this war was over,
with the Lakers,
even be playoff MVP).

Hal Greer didn't do so bad either in '67.
He led the champs with 27.2 points per game
in those 15 games,
ringing a bell for Philly.

Day 327: Rah rah!

Direct college actions
against the war
rose to 327
in the 1967-68 academic year.
That's up from 178 in 1964.
That means overt actions
specifically criticizing the war.
But including actions to protest
university complicity in the war,
the number reaches a robust 602.
That's up from none in 1964.
Probably before students realized how linked
their college and the government were.

Day 328: Running in

Because LBJ was faced with a choice
Because he was faced
Because the choice
Was being seen
Because it was a case
Of running in or running out,
And because he did not want to be
Because he did not want
To be seen running out,
He decided to run in.
Because he decided to run in,
He had McGeorge Bundy
Draft NSAM 328
In April of 1965.
NSAM 328
Authorized American personnel
In Vietnam
To take the offensive

Instead of just reacting,
To secure "enclaves"
And support ARVN troops
It meant sending in more troops.
Because not doing that
Would be running out.
Because.

Day 329: Rock Island East

In May of 1970,
when we sent troops into Cambodia,
in the Fishhook region,
guys from the First Cav
found a base so big
they named it Rock Island East, after Rock Island Arsenal
    in Illinois.
How big?
an estimated 329 tons of munitions,
probably the largest enemy cache found during the war.

Day 330: Playing another one

Record Group 330.
That's the Records of the Office of the Secretary of Defense
in the National Archives.
There's stuff there that can be looked up.
In case you were wondering.

Day 331: Operation Beef-Up

Our ranks they are so very thin,
Said CINCPAC to S o D.

We need three hundred, thirty-one more,
To boost M A A G.
It is September, 'sixty-two,
And I fear no light we'll see.

We've helped you more than double strength,
Replied the S o D.
We thought our forces adequate
For our role advisory.
Full seven hundred, thirty-four
Just came to you from me.

I know it looks like quite a lot,
Said CINCPAC to S o D,
But it's getting to be more than just
A role advisory.
We just can't get a handle on
Those folks we call VC.

Well here's the word you want to hear,
Said the S o D,
We'll call it Operation Beef-Up,
And expansion you will see,
And the name of that command will change
From Mag to the new MAC-V.

Day 332: Tiger tiger

The low weight range,
that's the low end,
for the male Indochinese tiger
is around 322 pounds.
(Give or take, but who's going to quibble
if you come face to face? Talk about a fearful symmetry.
Females are known to be lighter, if that makes you feel any better.)

That's the kind of tiger prowling Vietnam.
(You didn't know there were different kinds, did you?)
There were stories about these things stalking GIs on patrol.
Who knows if they were true?
I mean, an enemy soldier is bad enough,
but one of these guys?
And suppose he hasn't eaten for a few days?
An M-16 doesn't seem likely to stop one.
Might have to call in the artillery.

Day 333: Back at home again

With 333 yes votes,
the U.S. House of Representatives
approved
"An act to enforce the fifteenth amendment to the Constitution
    of the United States, and for other purposes,"
fondly known as the Voting Rights Act,
on July 9, 1965,
with 85 voting against it.
It had been approved by the Senate
(77-19, not as good as the Gulf of Tonkin, but what the hey)
in May.
President Johnson signed it in August.
Even Republicans voted for it.
But that was 1965.

Day 334: POWs

One of the pressing concerns
at home
was worrying about
prisoners of war.
At least if a family knew

its loved one was a POW,
there was hope.
But many families had no information,
nor did the government.
In early 1970,
Hanoi released a list of 334 POWs to an American antiwar group.
The U.S. government said the list was inaccurate.
Hanoi released a "definitive" list of 339 later in the year.

Day 335: Stalemate

With 335 words,
on February 27, 1968 (that year again),
Walter Cronkite,
beloved, trusted,
reassuring,
said that he didn't think the United States
could achieve any kind of victory in Vietnam
and could hope only for a stalemate, at best.
This shook many people,
who thought they could count on Walter
to tell them how well things were going,
and how well things were going to go,
which he had done earlier.
But what he saw and heard
by this time
wouldn't allow him to do that.
It isn't true
that LBJ was watching the broadcast and made his comment,
"If I've lost Walter Cronkite I've lost the country";
but there was some truth to the idea anyhow.

Day 336: Celluloid heroes: Training films

We're working with an approximate number here,
because the criteria can vary,

etc., etc., etc.,
but 336 movies were made
in the USA alone,
about World War II,
The Big One,
WW2.
It was the war
about which
so many participants
felt a great deal of pride.
It was the war
that was drummed into the minds
and hearts
of so many of the young men
who would fight in Southeast Asia
twenty or so
years later.
The war they would hear
and see
so much about.
The heroes
and the battles
and of course
the satisfying,
not to mention triumphant,
outcome.
And that's not counting the television shows.

Day 337: ... and influence people

In 1956,
the Eisenhower administration
offered $337 million in development funds
and $1 billion in military aid
to developing countries

in Latin America,
Africa,
and Asia,
in an attempt to offset
$1 billion given by the Soviets
in foreign aid credits.
Domestic critics
branded the program
an attempt to buy friends.
Well, duh.

Day 338: More casualties

338 is the number given
of Americans killed
in Operation Toan Thang 43,
the incursion into Cambodia
in April of 1970.
In the name of trying to end the war,
it expanded it,
the largest tactical operation involving U.S. forces
in over a year.
It might have set back
North Vietnamese operations by a year,
but it didn't achieve much else,
and, unhappy omen,
the ARVN did not perform well at all.
It caused a lot of criticism,
including in Congress,
and on college campuses.
338 American service members dead
in that month.
And did we mention four dead in Ohio,
and two dead in Mississippi?

Day 339: Diamond hero

With a .339 batting average
Roberto Clemente led the National League
in 1964.
He had already won it in 1961
and would win it again in 1965 and 1967.
he finished with 3,000 career hits, exactly,
but would never get another one
because he died in a plane crash,
on the last day of 1972,
not in southeast Asia
but trying to help earthquake victims in Nicaragua.

Day 340: Skyhawk

340 miles
was the range
of the Douglas A-4 Skyhawk,
the Navy's primary light bomber over North Vietnam.
It was flown by Everett Alvarez,
the first Naval POW,
and John McCain,
also a POW and, later, U.S. Senator,
and James Stockdale,
the highest-ranking Naval POW
and winner of the Medal of Honor.

Day 341: The man, the trail, the campaign

The North Vietnamese
had a 341st Division.
It was one of three
as part of the Ho Chi Minh Campaign,

which started in April of 1975.
They attacked and occupied
a town called Xuan Loc,
thus opening the way to Saigon
and the end of the war.
And the next day,
Nguyen Van Thieu
(who you remember from Day 231)
resigned as president of his country.
And the last blow in the defense of Xuan Loc
was an air strike by the ARVN air forces,
dropping CBU-55s, which were meant to clear mine fields.
And 341 was the number of headquarters
the North Vietnamese said
were hit by those CBU-55s,
thus suffocating or incinerating
more than 250 people.
They accused the South Vietnamese
of flouting all norms of morality.

Day 342: Have you looked under the chaise longue?

In 1954,
the U.S. Military Assistance Advisory Group, Vietnam,
or MAAG,
later to become MACV,
(as you will recall from days 20 and 331, et al)
was 342 men,
as limited by the Geneva Accords
(as you will recall from days 17 and 315).
In May of 1956,
Ike sent 350 men,
supposedly to help the South Vietnamese recover
equipment left by the French.

Considering how long we stayed there,
that must have been some equipment.

Day 343: Regional forces

The ARVNs had
a regional force battalion,
Battalion 343.
It was one of four,
along with 340, 342, and 367,
defending Xuan Loc.
Yeah, that Xuan Loc.
These guys weren't as successful
as their counterparts
of two days earlier.

Day 344: Batting champs

Ted Williams and Mickey Mantle,
the Splendid Splinter and the Commerce Comet,
both connected, in their own ways,
to the Yankee Clipper,
but both also connected with 344.
The Kid had a .344 lifetime batting average.
The Mick had 344 lifetime doubles.
They faced each other for ten seasons,
battling for MVP honors
(Mantle, 1957)
and battling titles
(Mick in '56, Ted in '57 and '58).
Ted retired in 1960;
it seems at 42 he was too old,
the same year that JFK,
who also had a Boston connection,

at 43 was too young.
Ted played in but one World Series, and lost,
but Mick played in twelve and won seven.
And that Yankee dynasty of which he was such an important part
won a Series in 1962,
his last Series victory
and the team's last until this war was over.
The Babylonian Captivity III.
Talk about a long, hard slog.

Day 345: Full accounting

Dec. 24, 2010

Dear Francisco,
I hardly know how to address a letter
to a brother I never really knew
and can hardly remember.
I write this letter every year,
on the day our mother learned
That you were killed in Vietnam,
a country I know almost nothing about.
For years,
the government said that
345 Puerto Ricans were killed in Vietnam
making you one of a small number.
And for years our people
argued that the number was larger.
So now we know for sure,
the official number is 455.
So should we celebrate the change?
I don't think you would fear
being lost among a larger group,
and at least our people are being recognized
for their part in a war
that no one wants to remember.

I want to remember you,
but my friends tell me
not to drive myself crazy
wishing for the impossible.
So I will look at the picture of you
in your uniform
and hope
that will keep you alive in my heart
and that there was a place for me in your heart.

Your loving sister,

Analisa

Day 346: Keep 'em rollin'

During Operation Rolling Thunder,
from about 1965
to the end of 1966,
the U.S. dropped 165,000 tons
of bombs on North Vietnam
destroying 346 (give or take)
fixed structures
and thousands
of railroad cars,
motor vehicles
and water craft.
The estimated military damage
was $200 million.
And still they kept on fighting.

Day 347: Tuition/The Cost of Learning

Dear Son,
I hope you are well.

We are fine here.
Your father sends
his best wishes.
I tell him he should write,
and he keeps saying he will,
but you know how he is about showing his feelings.
As I think you know,
your cousin Dan
is staying with us
for a while.
We are happy to have him,
and he seems more comfortable here
—or maybe less restless—
than he did at home.
He's using the spare room,
not yours,
please be assured of that.
Dad and Uncle Ed
rigged up a platform
so Dan can get his wheelchair in and out.
It's got a motor,
So he can move it with his good hand.
He signed up to go to college in the fall.
It will cost $347,
between tuition and books.
I would have thought it would be an even number,
and I had no idea it cost so much,
but he says his GI Bill money
and disability payments
will more than cover that.
When someone asked him what he'll take up,
He said "Space."
We told him he could live here,
But he says it would be better for him to live on campus.
He said he's lucky that he has all five fingers
on his right hand, so he can take notes

And not feel bad about raising his hand.
We told him that his left hand
with three fingers
doesn't look so bad,
but I don't think he believed us,
but it really doesn't look so bad.
He watches the TV news
every night,
just watching what they have about Viet Nam.
Your Dad watches with him,
even though he never watched it before.
I tried to watch with them,
but I can't,
because it makes me worry even more about you.
Dad tried to get him to go to the Legion hall.
He told him he could get cheap beer,
but he wasn't interested.
Dan doesn't go to church,
and one night he said
he doesn't believe in God.
I hope that's not true
and that maybe he's just depressed.
I don't know if I should ask our minister
to talk to him.
He sends his best
and said to watch where you step
and not to bring home a wife.
I don't care if you do that
just as long as you come home safe.
Please take care of yourself,
and write soon.

Your loving,

Mom

Day 348: And the beat goes on

Vietnam is a country
that has known
little more than war.
It was about
348 years
from Trinh-Nguyen war,
(see Day 22)
until 1975,
when the U.S. was gone for good.

Day 349: Peacetime benefits

In February of 1975,
President Ford submitted
a $349.4 billion budget
for fiscal 1976.
It meant a $51.9 billion deficit.
Ford forecast a deep recession,
high inflation,
and high unemployment.
He explained it as a peacetime deficit.

Day 350: Forest of Assassins

There was a place down near the Mekong Delta,
called the Rung Sat swamp.
"Rung Sat" coming from something
meaning "Forest of Assassins."
Supposedly it was an ancient pirate haven.
It was big,
but we set out about 350 acres
called the Rung Sat Special Zone.

It was a good hiding place,
for the enemy,
but we had combined Navy and Army operations
to keep things going smoothly for us
and not so smoothly for them.

Day 351: Heavy metal

North Vietnam
(the enemy, to us)
had a "heavy" division,
the 351st Artillery Division.
Its history went back a ways,
but in 1955, units of it were re-designated
with other numbers
to defend Hanoi from the French.
It gets heavy in 1960,
when it was organized
into artillery regiments and antiaircraft regiments.
Just in case you were wondering.

Day 352: What you'll need

352 hours.
The hours, the hours.
That's how many
hours of instruction
a trainee received
in infantry AIT.
The hours, the hours.
Being taught to use
all those weapons,
so useful in war,
so prevalent in peace.

The hours, the hours.
Even map reading.
And the alphabet,
radio style.
The hours, the hours.
To prepare young men
(and now even women, but not then)
for combat.
But the ones who were going to Vietnam,
they could get an extra week
to prepare them for the struggle.
The hours, the hours.
Going out there to Peason Ridge
to get a close look
at a fortified VC village.
The hours.

Day 353: Covering the base

Base Area 353
was a North Vietnamese installation in Cambodia.
It was one place
that was to be hit
in the (not so) secret bombing of Cambodia
Nixon ordered in March of 1969.
That order was meant,
in part,
as retaliation for a February 22 VC offensive
that Nixon said violated
unwritten agreements
between the USA and North Vietnam.
Base Area 353 was a base for
what we called COSVN,
or Central Office for South Vietnam,
North Vietnam's Cambodia-based headquarters,

which they called the Central Committee Directorate for the South,
but no matter what it was called,
conducted much of the war in South Vietnam.

Day 354: So then, back home, to Vietnam

On June 29 and 30, 1970,
U.S. ground combat troops
ended two months of operations
in Cambodia
and returned to Vietnam.
American military officials reported
354 Americans killed in action
and 1,689 wounded.
The ARVN reported 866 of its soldiers
killed in action
and 3,724 wounded.
There was no word on NVA/VC casualties.
What, no body count?
How are the folks back home supposed to know we're winning
    the war?

Day 355: Rough estimates

American and South Vietnamese estimators
estimated
that VC units
killed an
estimated
355 people
in a series of coordinated attacks
from the northeastern provinces
to the Mekong Delta
in August of 1967.

Heaviest casualties were in
the cities of Cantho and Hojan.

Day 356: Guests of the (not quite) nation

356 aviators
were prisoners of the North Vietnamese
at one point in 1970.
A survey showed the average POW
to be 32 years old, an Air Force captain
or Navy lieutenant,
married,
and with two children.

Day 357: Celluloid heroes, Part 2: Debriefing

357.
This number could change at any time
(and probably will),
But this is the approximate number of movies
about Vietnam, and wars that occurred in it.
Yeah, that many.
This doesn't mean just
what took place
from 1965 to 1975,
but going back more than that.
Like, for example,
Saigon,
with Alan Ladd
and Veronica Lake.
(I don't remember any women who looked like Veronica Lake
      over there.)
That movie came out in 1948.

Day 358: Keeping track of the casualty count

On August 27, 1970,
the U.S. command reported
that 358 GIs were wounded
and 52 were killed
the week of Aug 16-22.
That would make it
the lowest casualty toll
since the week of December 3, 1966.
That's at least the right direction.
Isn't it?

Day 359: Keep on truckin'

About 359 miles of bypasses,
171 miles of main road,
1,835 miles of vehicle-capable roads,
and 450 entry roads and storage areas.
That was what the Ho Chi Minh Trail
(or Truong Son, as the natives called it)
had at the end of 1967.
A June, 1966,
estimate by
the US Defense Intelligence Agency
(or DIA)
said that the North Vietnamese had
600 miles of truckable roads,
200 of which were good
for year-round use.
So,
did the Ho
find a way to grow,
or did our intelligence come in a little low?

Wouldn't be the first time to do so,
y'know?

Day 360: Joy in Mudville, or full circle, as it were

There was a crew of 360
on the USS C. Turner Joy,
when it was sent to assist
the USS Maddox
at the Gulf of Tonkin
on that fateful day
in 1965.

Day 361: Capital idea

Some scholars believe
(and who are we to disagree with them?)
that 361 men voted
to execute Socrates,
(and 140 voted not to).
Soc swallowed the poison
because not doing so
would have proven his enemies right
and, predating Bartleby,
he would prefer not to do that.
He could have defended himself
with appeals to the emotion
instead of to reason,
but
he would prefer not to do that either.
He was condemned
for corrupting the youth of his time.
It seems he wanted to question,

and wanted those youths to question,
how they knew
they knew
what they knew.
Yeah, that'll do it.

Day 362: Yet more hearts and minds, northern version

A North Vietnamese document
says that the U.S.
bombed 29 village infirmary-maternity houses,
a total of 362 beds,
in 1965.
Stopping them before they get started?
God, when is this going to be over?

Day 363: Serious shoveling

You think you've done a lot of digging?
Beginning on the Hudson River
and running along the Mohawk,
the Erie Canal,
which took from 1817 to 1825 to build,
was 363 miles long.
It revolutionized the freight business
and helped open the way
to the Midwest from the East.
It was 40 feet wide
and four feet deep,
and it had 83 locks
and 18 aqueducts.
Because of rerouting
through Lake Oneida,

it is 340 miles long now,
but you don't get any time off for that.

Day 364: Can't be cruel

One day left to go.
Keeping our heads down,
trying to be secure in the knowledge
that Elvis had 364 Number One albums.
And the year wouldn't be complete
without one last mention of the King,
now, would it?
He survived the Army,
but couldn't survive his own life.
We just have to survive one more day.

Day 365: Homeward bound

Flight 365.
Arriving from somewhere
into Bien Hoa.
Eagerly anticipated,
gratefully welcomed.
365 people step off.
365 uniforms,
365 duffel bags,
730 boots walking down the stairs
and hitting the ground one at a time,
walking forward.
Not marching, walking
Hesitantly.
Into the heat.

And flight 365 turns around and heads home.
It becomes flight Echo, tyoo, fower, zeero, yankee.

E240Y.
And 480 boots
stomp up the ramp
eagerly,
and 240 combat-tested, battle-weary,
happy-as-shit-to-be-getting-the-fuck-out-of-there people.
240 uniforms,
240 duffel bags
take their places for the flight
to Guam, Manila, Honolulu, Oakland, home.
And as E240Y leaves the ground
a cheer goes up.
a cheer from the 240
who are going home.

Day 365 and a half: We have met the enemy...

Start: Reception Center, Fort Dix, Saturday night.
The same place where, brand new, they gave them gloves in July,
now, used, just returning from a tropical climate in January,
they give them summer-weight dress greens.
And then send them on their way.
The cabbies circling around say, "I'll take you to Philly."
But four of them didn't want to go to Philly.
They wanted to go to New York.
So the cabbie said, "I can take you to New York.
It'll cost $100 for the ride.
You get five guys, it's $20 each; if it's only four guys
it's $25 each. Either way, it's $100 for the ride."
So they paid $25 each up front.
For a ride to Times Square: Finish.
And as the cab drove away,
proudly displayed in his back window:
the American flag.
Support the troops.

Acknowledgments

I would like to offer my thanks to people who helped bring this year of days into the light of day.

First of all is the publisher, and all-around good person, Matt Sinclair. I also want to express my thanks to Wes Davis and Terry Byrne for their advice and encouragement, to the Hartunian family for the Russian translations, and to Barry Levine for the tip about Skull Murphy's living arrangements.

Most of all, I would like to thank Edna, Meghan and Dave, Anne and John, and Julie, for helping me see that there are good days in this benighted world, and that there just might be many more good days to come.

About the author

Don McNamara served in the First Infantry Division in Vietnam from January of 1967 to January of 1968.

He is retired and lives in rural New Jersey.

We hope you enjoyed reading *Which the Days Never Know: A Year in Vietnam by the Numbers*.

Please consider sharing your thoughts about the book in a review on websites where books are discussed, such as Amazon or Goodreads.

It need not be long; an honest review is what says the most to other readers. Good, bad, or indifferent, all reviews are greatly appreciated.

And if you'd like to learn more about upcoming books from Elephant's Bookshelf Press, please sign up to receive updates at www.elephantsbookshelfpress.com